"In recent years, the study of parental alienation has become an enormously complex topic addressed in hundreds of books, scholarly chapters, and papers in academic journals. A parent who finds herself or himself alienated from a previously loving child may quickly feel overwhelmed by the vast amount of professional and amateur advice that is available. Amy J. L. Baker and Paul R. Fine have found a way to help alienated parents quickly—by focusing on five specific strategies by which a former spouse may cause parental alienation."

—**William Bernet, MD,** professor emeritus at Vanderbilt University School of Medicine, Nashville, TN

"This book provides the reader with much needed support as well as specific and helpful advice about how to parent a child who is involved in his parent's conflict. Every child deserves to love and be loved by both parents, and this book will help targeted parents achieve that goal."

—**Jason Patric**, actor, targeted father, and founder of *Stand Up for Gus*

"*Co-parenting with a Toxic Ex* is an excellent book for any parent dealing with a high-conflict co-parent in a separation or divorce. Baker and Fine accurately describe the hidden patterns of manipulation by a toxic ex that can lead to an alienated child—one who wants to avoid the other parent. Most important, they teach what to do and what not to do to protect a healthy parent-child relationship for the other parent regardless of these manipulations. This is a minefield and they provide supportive strategies and numerous tips for a reasonable parent to use—including how to avoid getting angry, giving up, or giving in."

—**Bill Eddy**, lawyer, therapist, and author of *Don't Alienate the Kids!: Raising Resilient Children While Avoiding High Conflict Divorce* (www.HighConflictInstitute.com)

"While *Co-parenting with a Toxic Ex* is technically not classified as a workbook, divorce *is* work, and often becomes a full time job. Amy J. L. Baker and Paul R. Fine have developed a chapter-by-chapter playbook for parents in any stage of divorce. The book encourages parents to bring strong parenting skills to the table while trying to create a solid foundation for the identity, growth, and maturity of their children. This dynamic duo does it again for so many parents struggling to find their way through the maze of co-parenting after divorce. Bravo!"

—**Jill Egizii**, president of the Parental Alienation Awareness Organization, USA

Co-parenting *with a* TOXIC EX

What to Do When Your Ex-Spouse Tries to Turn the Kids Against You

AMY J. L. BAKER, PhD

PAUL R. FINE, LCSW

New Harbinger Publications, Inc.

Publisher's Note

This publication is designed to provide accurate and authoritative information in regard to the subject matter covered. It is sold with the understanding that the publisher is not engaged in rendering psychological, financial, legal, or other professional services. If expert assistance or counseling is needed, the services of a competent professional should be sought.

Distributed in Canada by Raincoast Books

New Harbinger Publications, Inc.
5674 Shattuck Avenue
Oakland, CA 94609
www.newharbinger.com

Cover design by Sara Christian
Acquired by Melissa Kirk
Edited by Will DeRooy

Library of Congress Cataloging in Publication Data on file

FSC
www.fsc.org
MIX
Paper from responsible sources
FSC® C011935

RAINFOREST ALLIANCE CERTIFIED

Printed in the United States of America

16 15 14

10 9 8 7 6 5 4 3 2

We dedicate this book to our parents and our children, from whom we have learned so much about love, respect, and compassion; and to parents and children affected by alienation and loyalty conflicts. May they always be in each other's hearts.

Contents

Acknowledgments

We gratefully acknowledge the wonderful team at New Harbinger, including Melissa Kirk, Jess Beebe, and Nicola Skidmore, who create a collaborative writing and editing process, as well as copy-editor Will DeRooy. The book has been greatly improved through their loving attention to its words and meaning. We also would like to thank Andy Ross, who kindly assisted us at critical junctures with his ad hoc literary agent skills.

Introduction

Feeling as if you're losing your child to your ex is undoubtedly one of the most difficult experiences you may ever go through as a parent. If this is happening to you—if your child seems to feel and act as if she must love only one parent (your ex) and only one parent (your ex) can love her—you're probably missing your child terribly and mourning the lost opportunities to shape and guide your child and to watch her learn, grow, and develop. Moreover, losing your child to a "toxic" ex, one who's trying to turn your child against you, usually involves seeing your child become distant, cold, rude, selfish, and entitled, which can be extremely painful—one parent described the experience as like watching a monster eat her child alive, slowly—because no matter how badly your child behaves, she's still your beloved child, whom you cherish and want to protect. And, when a child is manipulated to unjustifiably reject one of his parents, he may suffer in the long run in terms of the way he relates to other people, his feelings about himself, and his ability to trust himself and others.

Many co-parents in your situation also suffer from being misunderstood and blamed by friends, family members, and others. Perhaps your friends and family members fail to fully understand what you're going through and aren't as supportive as you need them to be. Perhaps they don't understand your ex's insidious influence over your child and the inner conflict your child is experiencing that's causing his bad behavior. Perhaps they think you must have done *something* for your child to reject you so vehemently, since people often have a need to see the world as a just and rational place in which a child only rejects a parent who deserves it.

As a clinician (Paul) and a researcher and coach (Amy), we have found that popular advice to co-parents who seem to be losing a battle for their child's loyalty and respect seems to fall into one of two categories:

- "Take the high road and trust that your child will know which parent really loves him and has his best interests at heart."
- "Be tough on your child—don't let him get away with being disrespectful or using the divorce to manipulate you."

Unfortunately, not only is this kind of advice often unhelpful, but it can sometimes backfire, *worsening* your child's loyalty conflict or weakening your relationship with your child. It turns out that the best ways to counteract the efforts of an ex who's trying to turn your child against you aren't obvious and may not come naturally to many co-parents.

Helping you cope with your child who feels torn between you and your toxic ex is the goal of this book. We want to help you understand the five ways in which your ex might draw your child into a loyalty conflict, so that you can recognize them immediately and take appropriate action. We also want to help you understand the psychological impact of your ex's behavior on your child, so that you can be empathic and sensitive to your child's experience.

We believe that positive and mindful parenting will provide you with the tools that you need to help you strengthen your bond with your child. Being mindfully awake to your child, being compassionate in the face of her—and your—struggle with the divorce, and being self-aware will help you appreciate every moment with your child, as well as prevent unnecessary conflict. The tools throughout the book are designed to help you reduce your ex's negative influence and delay, if not prevent, your child from choosing your ex over you.

We wish you the best on your journey of discovery and healing, and we encourage you to keep in your heart and mind that your child needs you, even if she's not always able to remember it or act on that knowledge.

A Note on Language

While we recognize that many readers may never have been married in the first place or may not have finalized their divorce, for simplicity's sake we use the term "divorced" throughout this book. In addition, although you may be co-parenting more than one child, we decided to use the phrase "your child," singular. Finally, we consider *anyone* parenting with their ex to be a "co-parent." (Some writers reserve the term "co-parent" for the ideal co-parenting relationship, in which parents have a cooperative arrangement and treat each other with respect.)

1

Causes and Consequences of Loyalty Conflicts in Families of Divorce

Divorce isn't easy. The end of a marriage, especially in a family with children, brings a great deal of loss and change. You may have lost the family home, some of your income, some of your friends, and much more, or you may be at risk of losing many such things you once took for granted. Doubtless one such thing is your spouse's support of your relationship with your child. It can be very painful to realize that your former partner is now working against you in this regard.

Not all co-parents try to undermine their ex and steal their child's heart and mind. But too often they do. Yours might. And if that happens, your child may become caught up in a loyalty conflict.

What a Loyalty Conflict Is

A loyalty conflict occurs when a person feels that he must choose between two people rather than having a relationship with both of them, because of their antagonism toward each other. If your child is experiencing a loyalty conflict involving you and your ex, your child essentially feels as if she's in the middle of a tug-of-war, with one parent pulling on each arm, trying to bring her over to that side. In this situation, your child may feel as if he has to give up a relationship with you in order to please your ex. This is something to avoid at all costs.

Exercise 1.1: Recall Your Own Loyalty Conflict

Close your eyes and think back to when you were a child. Picture yourself at roughly the same age as your child is now. Can you think of a time when you experienced a loyalty conflict, either between your parents or between two friends? What did that feel like for you? What did you think and feel as you tried to cope with that? How was the situation resolved? Did you choose one side and relinquish the other, or did you manage to maintain a relationship with both individuals? How easy or hard was that? Write your reflections in the following space (or in a journal or notebook).

____

____

____

____

____

If you were able to recall a loyalty conflict that you experienced as a child, you probably had thoughts and feelings that revealed that it's not easy to be in the middle and feel that you have to choose a side. You might have thought: *I'm just a kid. Please don't put me in the middle. This isn't fair! I don't want to choose.* That's probably how your child is feeling, and for good reason. The situation is *not* fair; and it *is* painful, for a number of reasons.

How Loyalty Conflicts Harm Children

Loyalty conflicts in families of divorce cause stress and worry, create pressure on children to choose a side, cause children to experience confusion about the worth of their parents, and teach children unhealthy ways of relating to people. If your child does choose a side, this can be problematic as well.

Stress and Worry

When children feel pulled in two different directions by their parents, they know that to please one parent is to hurt or anger the other. There's no way to please both parents at the same time. This can lead children to worry about how they should respond to a variety of situations. Imagine that your child knows that both you and your ex will attend his upcoming performance at school. Will your child be able to focus on preparing for his performance? Will he be able to relax and enjoy himself on stage? Probably not. Instead, he'll be worrying about how to please both you and your ex, and dreading what will happen if he somehow slights one of you. When children experience this sort of undue stress, they may develop headaches, stomachaches, tension, lack of energy, and other physical symptoms. They may also experience emotional problems, such as anxiety or depression, and develop behavioral problems, such as social withdrawal or disobedience.

Pressure to Choose a Side

When your ex makes disparaging comments about you, impinges on your parenting time, or makes statements that lead your child to believe that she can't love both of her parents, your child may feel pressure to choose your ex and reject you. Children experiencing a loyalty conflict involving their parents are—whether they know it or not—under pressure. They may decide to choose one parent and reject the other simply to end the unpleasant feeling of being pulled in opposite directions. Sometimes this seems like the easiest solution, even though it causes more problems in the long run.

Confusion About Worth of Parents

If your ex is continually putting you down and creating situations in which your child will see the worst in you, your child may come to believe that you're truly unworthy and someone to be rejected and discarded. This can be very confusing to your child, who still needs you and has his own positive experiences of you, which may conflict with the messages that he's receiving.

Children need to believe that their parents love them. If your ex puts you down and tries to show your child how unloving you are, this hurts your child, who is likely to think that the reason you're not more loving is because she's somehow not good enough. Blaming themselves is one way that children can feel in control of a difficult situation, even if it leads to bad feelings about themselves.

Children also need to believe that their parents are good people. Believing that one of their parents is unworthy or inferior hurts children because they know that a big part of *them* comes from that parent. They may conclude, "If (Mom/Dad) is no good, and (Mom/Dad) is part of me, I must be no good as well." In this way, to turn a child against one of his parents is to turn a child against himself.

It may also be confusing for your child if your ex behaves in a way that suggests that your ex cares more about having his or her own needs met than about your child's need to love and be loved by both parents. It's as if your ex is saying to your child, "When you show me that you love your other parent, I feel hurt and angry," which could lead your child to feel that it's her responsibility to worry about and take care of your ex. This is obviously an unfair burden to place on a child.

Choosing a Side

When children *do* give in to the pressure to choose a side, this can lead to problems for them both in the short run and over the course of their lives. For one thing, they have lost a relationship with someone who can provide them with unique and valuable benefits. In other words, no matter which parent wins the loyalty conflict, the child always loses, because to be nearer to one parent is to be farther from the other. Second, they have given up their ability to think for themselves. They have traded in their own thoughts and perceptions for those of the parent with whom they have become aligned. They have adopted that parent's opinions, views, and beliefs. This dependency will ultimately make it hard for them to deal with peer pressure, make their own career choices, and become self-sufficient adults. Third, if a child eventually realizes that he was wrong to choose one parent over the other, he may suffer from guilt, low self-esteem, and depression later in life. Adults who as children rejected one of their parents in response to a loyalty conflict may say things like "I'm a terrible person for doing that to my father" and "When I think about what I did to my mother, I feel so sad I can't get out of bed in the morning" (Baker 2007; Baker and Ben Ami 2011).

Unhealthy Relationship Styles

If your child is caught up in a loyalty conflict involving you and your ex, she may—with your ex's encouragement—disrespect you and become insensitive to your feelings, which could result in her behaving in an entitled, ungrateful, and uncaring manner. These behaviors and attitudes toward you can spill over into her relationships with other people. In this way, your ex is warping your child's social and moral compass and molding your child to hold beliefs and attitudes that will serve her poorly later in life—with friends, at school, and on the job (Baker 2007).

Exercise 1.2: Which Symptoms of a Loyalty Conflict Do You See in Your Child?

Place a check mark in the corresponding column to indicate how frequently your child exhibits the behaviors and attitudes described since the divorce. (Keep in mind that some of these symptoms could be due to other stressors.) If you're co-parenting more than one child, you may want to complete this exercise separately for each child. You can download additional copies of the exercise at http://www.newharbinger.com/29583.

	Never That I'm Aware Of	**Sometimes**	**Often**
My child seems anxious, seems depressed, or complains of physical symptoms such as headaches, stomachaches, or fatigue.			
My child seems to have self-esteem issues and doubts about whether he or she is truly loved by both me and my ex.			
My child seems confused about the value and worth of me or my ex.			

Differentiating Bad-Mouthing Your Ex from Helping Your Child

It can sometimes be difficult for co-parents to know the difference between behaviors that may be helpful to their children and those that may create loyalty conflicts. If your child feels disappointment, anger, or hurt toward your ex, you may worry that if you validate these feelings or comfort your child, you'll be guilty of creating a loyalty conflict.

Of course it's important to be empathic with a hurt or disappointed child; just be mindful of *how* and *why* you respond. Don't deny or minimize your child's feelings and perceptions. At the same time, be careful that you don't make him feel worse than he already does by getting caught up in putting down your ex or making yourself look good by comparison. If you add your own interpretation of events or fan the flames of your child's discontent, then you're pulling him into a loyalty conflict. We'll talk more about unintentionally inducing a loyalty conflict later in this chapter.

Why Co-parents Behave in Ways That Draw Children into Loyalty Conflicts

Why would anyone want to induce a loyalty conflict in a child, when it seems so mean? The truth is that for many co-parents, feeling as though they're the favored parent helps reduce feelings of jealousy, fear, guilt, shame, sadness, loneliness, anger, or narcissistic injury. Let's examine these feelings, because when you understand the feelings that may lead your ex to try to turn your child against you, you may be able to address them and thus reduce his or her need to feel like the favored parent.

Jealousy

Your ex may feel jealous of how close you and your child seem. Rather than taking pleasure and comfort in knowing that the child you share is fortunate enough to have a loving relationship with you, your ex may worry that something is lacking in his own relationship with your child. At a time when friends are choosing sides and family members typically ally with their own family, there might be a heightened sense of insecurity that is causing your ex to feel anxious when he sees the positive relationship you have with your child.

Your ex may also feel jealous of your parenting time. Every minute that your child is with you is a minute that she's not with your ex, and he may feel that loss sharply. Your ex may miss greeting your child in the afternoon as she comes home from school or tucking her into bed at night. Perhaps your child recently had a "first"—took her first steps, said her first word, had her first sleepover, saw her first movie—and your ex wasn't there to experience the joy and have a memory of the milestone to cherish forever.

Co-parents have every reason to feel jealous of each other's parenting time. When you were married, both you and your ex may have craved "me time" to read a book, take a nap, or just sit peacefully and think. Taking care of children is so time-consuming that most parents feel some desire for down time. But nothing can really prepare full-time parents (if your ex was one) for the feelings associated with the transition to seeing their children only on designated parenting days. Even if your ex only saw your child at dinnertime most days you were married, he may still feel a sense of loss at not seeing your child as much as he used to.

It's also natural for your ex to feel jealous if you have more money to lavish on your child, more friends and family members to help with child care, or a more flexible job that allows you to spend more time with your child. Money, friends, and free time are not necessarily evenly distributed following a divorce, and to your ex you may appear to have it easy. If you have recently entered a romantic relationship, this may also spark feelings of jealousy, as may the perception that you're recovering from the pain of the divorce more quickly. Feelings of jealousy are natural in divorce situations. It's how you deal with them that can make a difference in terms of pulling your child into a loyalty conflict.

Fear

There are many reasons why a newly divorced parent may be fearful. Parents have a strong desire to protect their children, and after divorce it may be unnerving to relinquish the control derived from seeing their children every day. Many go from feeling separation pangs to worrying that their children will change or be harmed while they're away.

Most likely, you and your ex have differences of opinion about parenting, with one of you being more lenient, one of you being more health conscious, one of you being more traditional, one of you being more academically oriented, and so on. It's nearly impossible for two parents to agree on every aspect of parenting. When you were married, your ex may have been able to have more influence concerning matters on which you disagree than she does now. Truth be told, you're probably less likely to accommodate her wishes now that the two of you are no longer married. And it's possible that your differences regarding parenting have become magnified since the divorce as each of you struggles with the loss of control that comes with having your child spend significant periods of time away. For some co-parents, this experience of loss of control evolves into an irrational fear that the other parent will somehow harm the child. These co-parents try to pull the child away from the other parent in order to "rescue" the child from imaginary dangers. Your ex may even be afraid that your child will be injured in your care. Or the danger may be that your child will stop loving her.

Another source of fear is financial. Some co-parents are afraid of having to contend with a diminished income after the divorce, and in response they may seek to preserve their finances by having more time with the children (and hence paying less in child support, or receiving more).

Guilt

Co-parents may suffer from guilt over the breakup of the marriage, knowing that divorce can be traumatic for children. There are other reasons to feel guilty as well, including being less attentive to the children or less patient than usual while preoccupied with legal and other divorce-related matters. All parents have moments of preoccupation or self-absorption that can result in self-recrimination later (e.g., "Why couldn't I just put my magazine down and watch my child while he was playing in the sandbox?") After divorce, parents may be even more distracted by concerns about finances, loneliness, change, and so forth. Let's say that your ex has difficulty focusing when reading your child a bedtime story. Later, when he thinks back to how his mind wandered, he may chide himself for not being more attentive. Other co-parents feel guilty for having fun when their children are away—they wonder, *What kind of parent am I that I barely think about my kids when they're not around?* Such feelings of guilt can lead your ex to want to reassure himself that your child still loves him. If he can make your child prove her love by choosing him over you, then he may feel reassured that he's not such a bad parent.

Shame

Some co-parents experience shame, not just over the end of the marriage but over any way that they feel that they're lacking as a parent (and we are all lacking, in some way or another). Your ex may feel embarrassed when your child approaches you first after a school play or soccer game. She may feel ashamed when your child asks to call you or see you during her parenting time. If your child talks about you enthusiastically or expresses longing for you, it might cause your ex to wonder whether there's something lacking in her as a parent. Like guilt, shame can lead your ex to encourage your child to show favoritism toward her, to reassure her that she's not that bad a parent. She might create situations in which it's likely that your child will feel pressured to show favoritism, as a way to make herself feel better about the ways in which she has fallen short.

Sadness

Your ex is likely to feel sad about not having the pleasure of his child's company on a daily basis. Again, every moment that your child is with you is a moment she's not with your ex. Parents who are separated from their children—for whatever reason—miss them and want to be with them. This is true even during planned separations, such as sleep-away camp or sleepovers. Most parents worry that they're missing out on the things their children do when they're not there, and most likely your ex is no exception. To not be with your child every day and to miss out on watching her grow and develop represents a big loss for your ex. As a way to cope, your ex might encourage your child to reassure him that she loves him best of all and will never leave him. If he can convince your child to prefer him over you, then he doesn't have to deal with the sadness and loss of being separated from her, as well as his uncertainties, which have been magnified by the divorce.

Loneliness

If your ex is used to being with your child every day, then your child's absence from the home may be very painful for her. Separation from your child may make your ex feel lonely and make her want to pressure your child to spend more time with her. For someone used to having a child in the home every day, waking up to an empty house can be very disconcerting. Assuming that your custody arrangement involves your child staying with you some nights, there will be days when your ex doesn't get to receive a warm hug from your child at night and hear the joyful sound of footsteps and giggles the next morning. When you were married, it probably would have sounded like a fantastic vacation to your ex to wake up to a quiet house and have a day to herself. But if your child's absence is imposed (as opposed to chosen), then it can feel terribly lonely.

Some co-parents are more able to cultivate a "life" separate from their relationship and role with respect to their children, but for those whose identity is wrapped up in being a parent, the loss of their children—even only part of the time—may be extremely painful. If your ex was a stay-at-home parent whose main responsibilities revolved around child care, not having a child to focus on can affect her sense of purpose and self-worth. She might try to ward off the loneliness by encouraging your child to spend as much time with her as possible, to pay attention to only her when the three of you are together (at transition times, school events, and so on), and to generally prefer her over you.

Anger

There's a lot to be angry about after a divorce. Your ex may be angry at himself or at you for precipitating the end of the marriage and letting the family down. He may be angry at "the system" for imposing a disagreeable parenting plan on him. He may be angry at you for having a better relationship with your child than he does, or for doing things that he perceives to be wrong or hurtful to your child. When people are angry, they don't always think things through as carefully as they should. Your ex's anger may be preventing him from controlling his baser impulses, such as to compete with you for your child's affection. Furthermore, your ex may deliberately set out to punish you for real or imagined misdeeds, and one guaranteed way to hurt you is to limit your time with and interfere in your relationship with your child. For some co-parents, the anger they feel is not just an impetus for rash actions, things done and said "in the heat of the moment;" intstead, it fuels a malicious plan to steal their children away from the other parent.

Narcissistic Injury

Some people experience the loss of a relationship (e.g., divorce) as a personal affront and can't tolerate the resulting threat to their sense of self. The typical response of people who suffer such a narcissistic injury, as it's called, is to devalue the other person, in order to preserve their sense of self. For example, if your ex's ego was bruised during the divorce, she may come to view you as worthless in order to not feel badly about the end of the marriage. In a case of "sour grapes," she may convince herself that she has no idea what she ever saw in you in the first place and that she's *glad* that the relationship is over. If your ex fails to find any redeeming value in you, it becomes difficult for her to understand why anyone else (such as your child) would want or need to have a relationship with you either. Such co-parents find it hard to separate their negative feelings about their ex from their beliefs about their ex's value as a parent.

Exercise 1.3: Which of These Emotions Do You See in Your Ex?

Your ex (and you) may be dealing with many strong emotions in response to the divorce. If your ex often acts on any of these feelings and desires by creating situations that compel your child to choose your ex over you, you're co-parenting with a "toxic ex" and are at risk of losing your child.

Place a check mark in the corresponding column to indicate how frequently you sense that your ex is experiencing the following emotions.

	Never	**Sometimes**	**Often**
Jealousy			
Fear			
Guilt			
Shame			
Sadness			
Loneliness			
Anger			
Narcissistic Injury			

We want to be clear that while some co-parents purposefully induce loyalty conflicts—out of a desire to punish their exes, for example—others induce loyalty conflicts unintentionally because they have gotten caught up in feelings of fear, loneliness, and the like, which create a distorted need to protect or control their children. Sometimes it's hard to tell whether a co-parent is intentionally inducing a loyalty conflict or not; and this doesn't really matter, as far as what you can do to make a positive difference—in other words, the advice we would give you would be the same in either case.

Potentially Triggering Situations

With all of these feelings swirling around, there are times when co-parents are especially likely to behave in ways that draw their children into loyalty conflicts.

Transition Times

Any time that you, your child, and your ex are in the same place is ripe for your ex to create a loyalty conflict in your child. This is especially true when your child is transitioning from one home to the other—that is, as your ex is either preparing to say good-bye to your child or greeting him after a separation. Feelings of loss and all the other emotions we've described) may be heightened preceding and following a separation. Furthermore, perhaps your ex has unresolved feelings toward you, such as feelings of love, hurt, sadness, or anger (over real or perceived misdeeds). Perhaps there's a new spouse or partner in the mix, adding to the level of tension and discomfort. In this hotbed of emotion, it's possible that your ex will—intentionally or otherwise—induce a loyalty conflict in your child. In some families of divorce, the parenting plan requires that transitions take place in the presence of both parents, allowing your ex to see just how close you are with your child (which may spark feelings of jealousy) and providing him with an opportunity to shape your child's perception of you through his words, attitudes, and actions toward you. Perhaps you have noticed your ex turn cold toward your child at these times, leading her to focus on pleasing him while disregarding your feelings. For example, if your child shows you affection, your ex acts hurt or standoffish, influencing her to refrain from such displays in the future. Or perhaps your ex makes derisive comments toward you, such as "So, you showed up! Congratulations for being on time," suggesting that you're worthless or that you don't love and cherish your child. Perhaps your ex has whispered to your child something like, "Remember to call me if you feel uncomfortable," sowing seeds of doubt about your parenting and fear about the potential for you to cause her harm. Or perhaps your ex acts in ways that keep your child's focus on him instead of you.

Other Times When the Three of You Are Together

You, your ex, and your child are likely to be together at your child's back-to-school nights, athletic events, dramatic or musical performances, birthday parties, and so on, as well as less joyful occasions such as emergency-room visits, hospitalizations, and funerals. These are obviously situations in which feelings run high—especially the types of feelings we have discussed—and in which your ex may be more likely to behave in ways that can induce a loyalty conflict in your child.

On such occasions, your ex may complain to your child about her having shown favoritism toward you in the past (whether it's true or not), in order to ensure that she'll favor *him* this time. For example, before your child's basketball game, your ex may gripe that your child usually sits with *you* during halftime. Like most children, your child probably doesn't keep track of such things, but will believe your ex regardless. Thus your child might tell you at the game, "It's only fair—I usually sit with you during halftime, so I'm going to sit with Dad for a change." Unless *you* have been keeping track, you may find it hard to protest.

When the three of you are together, your ex can see for herself just how much your child loves and is loved by you. This may trigger feelings of jealousy, shame, anger, and all the other emotions we mentioned. Furthermore, any time your child is watching you interact with your ex, your ex may model for your child negative ways of seeing and responding to you. In other words, your ex's negative attitude or behavior toward you can distort the image your child has of you. If for example your ex conveys her disdain for you or makes it appear as if something you said or did was ridiculous, harmful, or unloving, this may undermine your authority and devalue you as a parent in your child's eyes. Or your ex may behave as if you intend to harm her or your child, thereby creating the impression that you're dangerous and frightening. Or your ex may pointedly ignore you while monopolizing your child's attention, so that there's little chance for you and your child to connect, resulting in the loss of an opportunity to share a moment together.

Major Changes

If anyone in the family experiences a significant change, this could also trigger feelings of a loss of control in your ex that may lead him to induce a loyalty conflict. If you remarry, for example, your ex may feel especially insecure or vulnerable; if your ex remarries, he may feel empowered and entitled. If your child changes—for example, becoming more challenging or distant—your ex may feel worried that your child is slipping away from him. If your child takes up one of *your* hobbies or interests, this could feel like a loss of control and lead to feelings of anger. If your child has difficulties in school or is diagnosed with a learning disorder, this could also lead to feelings of anger, as if you somehow induced these problems.

In general, change is difficult, and divorce is challenging enough for most people, so any additional changes may be very unsettling. However, children are constantly changing: they take on new mannerisms, they develop new interests, their appearances change, and they acquire new knowledge and skills. While it can be joyous to watch your child grow and develop, it can also be unsettling for your ex to have your child return to him changed after spending time with you. This kind of change intensifies the feelings of loss and sadness that most parents experience as a natural response to their children's growth.

Milestones

When your child reaches a significant milestone that your ex doesn't have the opportunity to witness or participate in, it may trigger feelings of resentment, sadness, shame, anger, and jealousy. Many childhood "firsts," such as first steps, first haircut, first word, and first lost tooth, happen in the blink of an eye. For co-parents, there's no way—unless they're unusually cooperative and in frequent contact—for both parents to experience all of these "firsts." One parent gets more and one parent gets less; at least, that's how it can feel. If your ex is suspicious by nature, she may feel that you deliberately excluded her from an experience, triggering anger and resentment. She might then purposefully exclude you from comparable opportunities, to spite you or compete with you—for example, taking your child for her first haircut without discussing it with you, or taking your child to have her ears pierced even though you agreed to wait until she was older. Your ex may want to demonstrate that she has the power and control in this co-parenting relationship. She may want to make you feel left out and unimportant.

Exercise 1.4: How Stressful Are These Situations in Your Family?

The situations that can heighten your ex's desire to create a loyalty conflict in your child are summarized in the following table. Place a check mark in the corresponding column to indicate how stressful these situations usually are for you.

	A Little	Somewhat	Very Much
Transition times			
Other times when the three of you are together			
Major changes			
Milestones			

Conclusion

Loyalty conflicts occur in families of divorce when co-parents experience feelings that lead them to want their children to side with them against the other parent. When children are made to experience loyalty conflicts, they suffer in the short run and may actually cut off one parent—become alienated—as a result. When that happens, children take on a number of behaviors that differentiate them from children who reject one of their parents for a good reason. In the next chapter, we describe these behaviors, along with the five primary behaviors that co-parents use to induce loyalty conflicts in their children.

2

How Co-parents Create Loyalty Conflicts and How Children Respond

If your ex is experiencing some of the feelings discussed in chapter 1, then he may engage in one or more of the types of behaviors described next. If so, you're co-parenting with a toxic ex. Luckily, not every child exposed to these behaviors is so affected as to become alienated—but your child might be. Once caught up in a loyalty conflict, your child is likely to exhibit some if not all of the eight behaviors described later in this chapter.

After reading this chapter, you'll have a clearer sense of the ways in which your ex may be turning your child against you and the signs that your child is being affected. This provides the foundation for understanding the parenting strategies presented later in the book.

Five Behaviors That Co-parents Use to Induce Loyalty Conflicts

If your ex is trying to turn your child against you, he's probably using one or more of the following five behaviors, all of which have been identified in research with parents (Baker and Darnall 2006) and adult children (Baker 2007; Baker and Chambers 2011; Baker and Ben Ami 2011). These behaviors work with one another to create conflict and distance in your relationship with your child. Although we describe them briefly in this chapter, we'll do so in greater detail later in the book.

Sending Poisonous Messages About You

If your ex is sending your child poisonous messages about you, he finds fault with every aspect of your personality and conveys his disdain to your child through his words, attitudes, and actions. He exposes your child to a consistent stream of negativity, criticizing if not condemning every aspect of your personality and life. He even depicts your positive characteristics as problematic and cause for concern, if not outright contempt. He makes negative comments with a frequency and conviction that makes them believable. When your child hears these comments, she may come to believe things about you that aren't true. We'll discuss ways to respond when your ex is sending poisonous messages about you in chapter 5.

Interfering with Contact and Communication

If your ex is interfering with your contact and communication with your child, she systematically excludes you from opportunities to share and connect with your child. She makes it difficult for you to communicate with your child during separations. Your phone calls and your texts and e-mails are blocked or go unanswered. These behaviors work hand in hand with poisonous messages to weaken your relationship with your child. We'll discuss ways to respond when your ex is interfering with contact and communication in chapter 6.

Erasing and Replacing

If your ex is trying to erase you in the heart, mind, and life of your child, he minimizes your role in your child's life and creates a new history that exaggerates his own contribution to her upbringing. Erasure also involves referring to you by your first name instead of "Mom" or "Dad" and encouraging your child to follow suit, as if you were no more important than anyone else whom he would refer to by first name. Your ex may install a new partner as someone to take your place and refer to this person as "Mom" or "Dad." Your ex may remove your name and information from emergency-contact forms; not include your name and information when filling out new forms; or keep you from receiving important school, medical, and extracurricular documents and schedules. We'll discuss ways to respond when your ex is erasing and replacing you in chapter 7.

Encouraging Your Child to Betray Your Trust

If your ex is encouraging your child to betray your trust, she induces your child to keep secrets from you and spy on you. Spying may include keeping track of how much you spend, whom you speak with on the phone, and how much money you earn. Your ex probably uses persuasion and flattery—letting your child know how important and trusted he is—to get him to do her bidding. Your child justifies his betrayal of you by denigrating you, resulting in an entrenchment of his negative feelings toward you. We'll discuss ways to respond when your ex is encouraging your child to betray your trust in chapter 8.

Undermining Your Authority and Fostering Dependency in Your Child

If your ex is undermining your authority, he constantly speaks out against your house rules and erodes your value as a parent in your child's eyes. He finds ways to "rescue" your child from your rules, consequences, and punishments, while simultaneously imposing his own. If your child seems preoccupied with pleasing your ex and strictly follows his demands no matter the inconvenience to her or you, your ex may have instilled a desire in your child to please him at the expense of all other relationships. This will make it increasingly difficult for you to function as an authority figure. We'll discuss ways to respond when your ex is undermining your authority and fostering dependency in your child in chapter 9.

Exercise 2.1: How Often Is Your Ex Engaging in These Behaviors?

Place a check mark in the corresponding column to indicate how frequently your ex seems to use the behaviors that we've discussed.

	Never That I'm Aware Of	**Sometimes**	**Often**
Sending poisonous messages about you			
Interfering with contact and communication			
Erasing and replacing you			
Encouraging your child to betray your trust			
Undermining your authority and fostering dependency in your child			

Eight Signs That Your Child Is Caught Up in a Loyalty Conflict

Some children who have been exposed to the behaviors described in the previous section are able to stay out of the fray and maintain a relationship with both parents. They shrug and say to themselves, *I don't care what Mom and Dad say; I love them both.* Unfortunately, not all children are resistant to parental pressure. Some children get caught up in the intense emotions of the loyalty conflict and align themselves with one parent, becoming alienated from the other. This happens when one parent's loyalty-conflict-inducing behaviors are successful in doing both of the following:

- Driving a wedge between the child and the other parent, eroding the child's experience of that parent as safe, loving, and available
- Creating a cohesion or enmeshment between the child and the loyalty-conflict-inducing parent such that the child is unwilling or unable to experience a healthy and natural separation from that parent, due to fear of being abandoned by or disappointing him or her

The good news is that this change doesn't happen overnight. There are signs that a child is getting caught up in a loyalty conflict. These behaviors were first identified by child psychiatrist Richard Gardner (1998) and their existence has since been validated by other clinicians and researchers (e.g., Bernet et al. 2010; Baker, Burkhard, and Kelly 2012). Gardner observed loyalty-conflict behaviors in children who were the subject of custody disputes. Some of these children exhibited some of these behaviors some of the time, but were for the most part able to have a relationship with both of their parents. (These children were "mildly alienated.") Some of these children exhibited more of these behaviors more of the time and had greater difficulty going back and forth between their parents. (These children were "moderately alienated.") Children who exhibited most or all of these behaviors most of the time eventually refused all contact with one parent. (These children were "severely alienated.") If you keep a watchful eye out for these behaviors, you can intervene while your child is only mildly alienated rather than wait until your child refuses to have anything to do with you.

These behaviors are uncommon in most children, even those who have been abused by and thus have a legitimate reason to feel hurt by or angry with one of their parents (Briere 1992; Dutton and Painter 1981; Kempe and Kempe 1978). They're mostly seen in children who have been manipulated by one parent to falsely and unjustifiably reject the other parent. Keep in mind that alienated children may behave in a very unloving and hurtful manner, but this doesn't mean that they're evil or bad, only that they're caught up in a loyalty conflict and aren't able to be their best selves at this time.

A Campaign of Denigration

Usually, the first sign that your child has been affected by a loyalty conflict is that he becomes unreasonably negative toward you. He exaggerates minor flaws of yours and reacts to them as if they're signs of your unworthiness as a person and a parent. He behaves as if he's empowered and entitled to inform you of all the ways in which you have failed him, and he does so in a harsh and uncaring manner. He shocks you by speaking to you arrogantly and spitefully and condemning you coldly. One girl explained to her father that he was like an old watch. "It's like this," she blithely explained. "If I had an old watch and it stopped working, I would say, 'Oh well. Too bad.' That is how I feel about you. If you died, I would say, 'Oh well.'" What's so astonishing about this example, in addition to the girl's callousness, is that she actually had a loving relationship with her father.

A campaign of denigration usually includes provocative behaviors. Thus, even if he claims to be afraid of you abusing him, your child will actually behave rudely and abusively toward you, rather than fearfully. One child e-mailed her father and demanded that his new wife "clean her filthy house or you can forget about visitation this weekend!" Another child purposefully bumped into his father to knock him off balance and then accused the father of attacking him. As we have noted, this behavior is not typical of abused children; children with an abusive parent are more likely to try to appease, rather than provoke, that parent in order to avoid another outburst and possible harm.

When on a campaign of denigration, rather than making statements criticizing the things that you *do*, your child makes statements that criticize *you*. Instead of saying, "I don't like it when you drive so fast," or "I wish you would make something else for dinner other than pasta," your child tells you, "I don't feel safe with you," or "You never make me food I like." Furthermore, your child denies having had any positive experiences with you in the past and may go so far as to say, for example, that he was only smiling in those home movies because you made him and he wasn't having as much fun as he appeared to be. On a survey used to identify alienated children, Amy Baker, Barbara Burkhard, and Jane Kelly (2012) included a question asking children to recall one good memory of each parent. When asked about the rejected parent, the children in the study claimed to lack a single good memory. Some of the children wrote the word "NONE" in capital letters followed by more than a dozen exclamation points.

Finally, a campaign of denigration includes a willingness on the part of your child to broadcast to others, like neighbors, other parents, teachers, and coaches, his troubles with you. An example from research (Baker and Darnall 2007) concerns a child whose mother was running for the school board. The child wrote the mother's opponent a letter wishing her well because the mother was such a terrible person and deserved to lose the election. In divorce proceedings and family court, your child will ask—if not demand—to speak to the judge and will prepare for sessions with a custody evaluator or guardian ad litem, arriving with a long list of complaints about you and your faulty parenting. Your child will appear to take pleasure in telling the world just how horrible you are. This highly unusual behavior runs counter to most children's desires to keep family problems private. Even children who have been beaten or molested by one of their parents are generally reluctant to reveal the abuse, even to a trusted mental health professional. They don't want that parent to get into trouble, and they don't want to hurt or anger that parent. They don't even want to discuss the abuse because that would make it more real. What they want is for everyone to pretend that it never happened so that they can go on with their lives.

When a parent abuses a child, the child doesn't say to himself, *(Mom/Dad) really needs to brush up on (her/his) parenting skills.* Children typically see the problem as *their* fault. One reason this is so is because children are naturally egocentric. This doesn't mean that they're pathologically narcissistic, just that they're developmentally inclined to see themselves as the center of their experiences. So if one of their parents hits them, they'll think that they must have done something to deserve it, even if the parent doesn't say so. The way most children see it, they have no reason to be angry at or to complain about an abusive parent, and talking about or telling others about the problem would make *them* look bad. Furthermore, most children with an abusive parent want to remain with that parent to get a chance to make things right, because that would mean that they're not "bad" anymore. For this reason, it's highly unusual for children to broadcast that their parent is horrible, despicable, and abusive.

It's important to note that children—especially teenagers or those dealing with social, emotional, or behavioral problems—sometimes demonstrate rudeness, thoughtlessness, or contempt in the absence of a loyalty conflict. If both parents get their fair share of the blame and recrimination, such behavior is probably teenage rebellion or related to a different problem. But if it's always *you* on the receiving end of the hostility, it's probably related to a loyalty conflict.

The Effect on Your Child's Development

Needless to say, this behavior can be very damaging to your child's character formation and well-being. Rather than being taught forgiveness and charity, she's being taught harshness and cruelty. Rather than being taught how to work through problems and accept others' imperfections, she's being taught how to be demanding and how to walk away from people who displease her. She's being taught that people are expendable, and that anyone who displeases her should be treated with contempt and disdain.

Weak, Frivolous, or Absurd Reasons for Rejecting You

If your child who's on a campaign of denigration is asked why she's so angry with you, the rationale she gives may be out of proportion to the level of animosity she displays. In other words, your child may offer explanations that fail to account for her hostility toward or rejection of you. If, for example, a therapist asks your child "So, what's the deal? You used to live with your mother, but now you don't want to even have a cup of hot chocolate with her once a month?" the reasons she responds with may be weak (e.g., "I just don't feel comfortable being there anymore"), frivolous (e.g., "The wooden floors in her house are scratched," "Mom wears cowboy boots with skirts"), or patently absurd (e.g., "She locked me in a closet for three weeks and starved me," when there's evidence that your child attended school during that period and was seen daily having meals with the family). Or she may decline to answer in this instance, saying with exasperation, "I have already told you why I'm upset, and I don't feel like repeating myself." One father shared that his three-year-old son explained that he no longer wanted anything to do with him because he never let him nap on the couch. These kinds of explanations, which lack compelling reasons for your child's feelings toward you, reflect a serious disparity between the punishment, so to speak, and the crime.

Weak, frivolous, or absurd reasons for rejection reflect what one attorney refered to as "the pounce." Because all parents are imperfect, you were certain to make a mistake at some point. You might have been too harsh, too permissive, too preoccupied, and so forth. And when you slipped up, your toxic ex encouraged your child to pounce on this error as if it were "The Reason" the relationship must end, even though your child started slipping away from you well before that. It's almost as if your child was waiting for something to happen so that she could take down from the shelf a preplanned response of full-scale rejection.

In one case, the excuse for the pounce was the father's confiscation of the daughter's cell phone because she neglected to leave it in the kitchen at night, per the family rule imposed to prevent cell phone use after bedtime. The daughter became outraged, went to spend time with the mother "to cool off," and never returned. The mother was only too happy to harbor the daughter, purchase her another cell phone, and report to the father that the daughter was too upset to spend time with him. This father had done nothing more than exercise his parental authority. Little did he know that it would set off a full-scale rejection. One would think that—given the magnitude of the daughter's response—he had beaten her, or grounded her for a month, or taken the family on vacation and left her behind to clean the house!

In another family of divorce, following an argument between the mother and the daughter, the father flew in from his home out of state and brokered a deal to let the daughter stay with him to "cool off." A memorandum of understanding between the parties, detailing when the daughter would be returned, was signed. However, shortly after bringing her to his home state, the father enrolled her in school and refused to return her to the mother. This father and daughter pounced on the argument and leveraged it into a permanent transfer of custody.

Some children will allege physical or sexual abuse as their reason for not wanting to spend time with the other parent. In itself, an abuse claim is not a weak, frivolous, or absurd reason for rejection. Quite the contrary, an allegation of abuse must be taken very seriously. However, in some cases there's just no evidence to support the claim. In some cases, a claim is proven to be false (i.e., the abuse is alleged to have occurred at a time or place that the parent and child weren't together or in a manner that is not physically possible), but the child (and the ex) continue to cite abuse as a reason for the animosity. In any event, an allegation of abuse is a game changer. Once an abuse claim has been filed, child protection services may prohibit contact between the child and the alleged perpetrator while the claim is investigated. This allows the other parent unfettered access to the child and can certainly entrench the child's disaffection for the accused parent, even if the abuse never happened.

The Effect on Your Child's Development

Children who lie about or exaggerate the negative qualities of one parent in order to please the other are taught a very dangerous skill: how to manipulate the truth, and how to dissemble to advance one's cause at the expense of others. This is not a quality that most parents want their children to learn, and for good reason.

Lack of Ambivalence Toward You and Your Ex

Children have some ambivalence, or mixed feelings, about most of the people in their life. Your daughter may adore her BFF but still be frustrated when this friend acts like a tattle-tale or displays some other characteristic that annoys her. Your son might describe a favorite coach as "awesome" but still concede that this coach is a wacky dresser or has bad breath. A beloved teacher might be seen as having a corny sense of humor or being too hard a grader. In other words, your child can often hold good and bad feelings about the same person in her mind at the same time, whether that person is you, your ex, or anyone else. However, if your child is caught up in a loyalty conflict involving you and your ex, she may seem to have selectively lost this ability.

We wish to stress that all parents are imperfect. All parents have some flaw or some quality that could be annoying or frustrating to their children. Not only that, but even the most generous, flexible, and accommodating of parents must sometimes set limits that cause resentment and frustration. Children make all sorts of unreasonable requests. There's simply no way that a parent could or should grant a child's every wish. Children shouldn't eat cookies for breakfast, play outside after dark, have play dates every day after school, have a short-order cook at their disposal, ride their bike without a helmet, stay up until midnight, or sleep with their bedroom light on. In other words, being a parent involves sometimes saying no to your child. And your child will experience frustration—and perhaps even rage—on these occasions.

Fortunately, most children come to understand that parents aren't all-powerful and can't satisfy their every desire. Most children are able to understand that their parents are human beings who have strengths and weaknesses, good qualities and not-so-good qualities. If your child is caught up in a loyalty conflict, however, she may express no ambivalence about your ex, demonstrating an extreme, idealized support for him. She may behave as though she never has mixed feelings toward or negative reactions to him. Your ex may be made to seem all good, while you are all bad. As one alienated teen eerily proclaimed, "I love my father to death!" Such hero worship combined with baseless contempt for the other parent is unhealthy and unrealistic.

Keep in mind that because all parents are imperfect, the favored parent is also imperfect. In fact, the favored parent may have many quite obvious flaws—a quick temper, a drug habit, a disinterest in providing appropriate supervision—but these don't matter to the child who's caught up in a loyalty conflict. Whatever that parent does, the child perceives as good, simply because that parent did it. In one case, a mother who was the favored parent neglected to have a doctor examine her son after he sustained a painful sports injury. Later, when he finally received proper medical attention, it was determined that he had fractured a bone and would require a cast. This boy seemed unfazed by his mother's apparent lack of concern for his medical needs. In his eyes, her choice not to take him to the doctor straightaway must have been the right one. In many cases, the flaws of the favored parent objectively exceed those of the disfavored parent, but the child behaves as if it were the other way around. Your child focuses on *your* perceived negative qualities, while minimizing if not completely overlooking your ex's.

As noted earlier, the behavior of children who are caught up in a loyalty conflict is quite different from that of children who have been abused by one of their parents or have some other legitimate reason to reject him or her. Generally, abused children do not condemn the abusive parent, nor do they worship the non-abusive parent (Briere, 1992). They're able to express a full range of emotions toward both parents. For example, a sexually abused child might say, "I love my father, but I wish he didn't come into my bedroom at night," or a physically abused child might comment, "My mom is great except when she loses her temper—then I don't like her so much."

The Effect on Your Child's Development

Lack of ambivalence represents a distortion of reality and, as such, could eventually interfere with your child's development, well-being, and ability to function in the real world. Most people have good and bad qualities, and to believe that people are either all good or all bad is unrealistic and simplistic. A child who assumes that anyone less than perfect should be rejected is a child who will grow up to have few friends and a very hard time maintaining relationships and interacting in a mature and appropriate manner.

The "Independent Thinker" Phenomenon

If your child is caught up in a loyalty conflict, he may repeatedly assert that his negative feelings about you are completely his own and not in any way influenced by your ex. He may go out of his way to reassure you that your ex played no role whatsoever in his antagonism toward you. He might even invoke the concept of "free will," sounding and acting unusually grown-up. Yet, as in

Hamlet (act 3, scene 2—"The lady doth protest too much, methinks"), the need to affirm something so strongly may communicate your child's need to make himself believe it rather than its inherent truth. In other words, your child reveals your ex's influence by preemptively and fervently denying it.

The hallmark of the "independent thinker" phenomenon is not simply denial of the other parent's influence when asked but *anticipation* that someone might assume such an influence, spurring strenuous efforts to protect the favored parent from blame. For example, your child walks into the room and says (if you're the mother): "Mom, I came up with this idea all on my own, so don't bother being mad at Dad or thinking that Dad had anything to do with this, because he didn't. This is one hundred percent my idea that I worked out all on my own." Your child's defense of your ex will be followed by a litany of rehearsed complaints and borrowed scenarios (discussed later in this chapter) that justify his cruel and unnecessary rejection of you.

All of this can help your ex maintain a façade of wanting your child to have a good relationship with you while ensuring that it doesn't happen.

The Effect on Your Child's Development

Over the course of their development, children are typically taught how to think critically, how to problem solve, and how to determine their own truth. If your child is unduly influenced by your ex, his ability to think for himself is being compromised. He'll need (and be expected to need) your ex to make decisions for him regarding his preferences, his choices, and his plans. His free will has been pre-empted. All decisions, likes and dislikes, and plans and goals are filtered through the needs and desires of his other parent. Your child—while proclaiming to be making decisions for himself—is actually unnecessarily dependent on your ex, to the detriment of his ability to feel and experience his own thoughts and feelings.

Absence of Guilt for Rejecting You

Children who are drawn into loyalty conflicts involving their parents tend to treat one parent very badly. Essentially, they have been given permission by the other parent to break that parent's heart. If your child is caught up in a loyalty conflict, she may behave rudely and coldly toward you. Furthermore, she may appear to have no qualms about treating you in this manner. She may say things like "You don't deserve to see me" when discussing her decision to cut you out of her life. Gratitude for your gifts, your favors, or your affection may be noticeably absent. Your child may try to get whatever she can from you, believing that it's owed to her and that because you're such a contemptible person, you don't deserve to be treated with respect, gratitude, or even civility. Your authority as a parent has been denied and erased, and your child has been encouraged to treat you as if your feelings don't exist or don't matter.

An example of this behavior involves a child walking proudly out of family court after lying about his mother to the judge, declaring "I did it!" as if it were a tremendous triumph, gloating about his misdeed instead of expressing reluctance or hesitation. As we noted earlier, some children may behave in an entitled and ungrateful manner for other reasons. Such behavior is a sign of being caught up in a loyalty conflict only when it occurs in response to or in conjunction with exposure to behaviors that may induce a loyalty conflict and in the absence of a legitimate reason (such as abuse or neglect by the rejected parent).

Research on adults who behaved this way as children revealed that some of them did feel guilty at the time but were unable to show it for fear of the favored parent's disapproval. Many also experienced guilt later, once they realized how badly they had treated the parent whom they had so harshly rejected (Baker 2007).

Like the other signs of being caught up in a loyalty conflict, lack of guilt stands in stark contrast to the behavior of abused children, who often experience guilt when setting limits or protecting themselves from an abusive parent, bending over backward to see things from that parent's perspective rather than from their own.

Abused children are generally protective of their abuser and tend to feel badly if they do or say anything that would cause that person to get into trouble or be displeased with them.

> **The Effect on Your Child's Development**
>
> Absence of concern for other people is likely to interfere with your child's healthy growth and development. Without the experience of guilt for wrongdoing and without an awareness of or concern for others' feelings, your child won't have the internal checks and balances necessary to prevent him from behaving in a way that might hurt other people. A child who does not experience empathy could grow up to run roughshod over the needs and feelings of other people and will be unlikely to sustain meaningful, healthy relationships.

Reflexive Support for Your Ex in Parental Conflicts

Co-parents often disagree over decisions regarding the welfare of the children as well as ongoing adjustments to the parenting schedule. Once the court-ordered parenting plan has been finalized, there are still countless ambiguities in the plan that provide opportunities for disagreements about its implementation. What happens, for example, in a year when Mother's Day falls on the father's birthday? If Mondays are transfer days and the child has no school on a particular Monday, who "owns" that time—the parent who has the child during the school week, or the parent who has the child on weekends? It's doubtful that a parenting plan can cover every eventuality; there are always some gray areas. Toxic co-parents seem to possess a particular genius for zeroing in on those areas. Needless to say, such co-parents will make a case for why *they* should have the children during those times. The children may follow in lockstep, repeating the rationale as if it made sense even when it's patently absurd. For example, one father declared that although he usually was entitled to two weekends a month, if a weekend started at the end of a month and crossed into the next month it would automatically be his weekend because "one month bled into the next." Despite the absurdity of this notion, the child would readily agree and assert that, of course, the father had this additional parenting time due him.

Parenting time is not the only topic on which co-parents may fail to see eye-to-eye. They may also disagree about allocation of resources, how to handle milestone events that both parents have a reasonable expectation of participating in, and more. No matter what the disagreement is about, children who are caught up in a loyalty conflict will side with their favored parent. A particularly common disagreement between co-parents concerns the use of college savings. To give you an example of reflexive support for the favored parent, let's say a young child accuses one of his parents of stealing his college money. This child doesn't yet fully understand what college is or even the concept of money, but he makes the accusation because he heard it from the favored parent. The accused parent rushes to refute the claim, rifling through bank statements to find the most recent one and show it to the child. The assumption is that the child will be interested in seeing evidence that the accusation is false. However, nothing could be further from the truth. Rather than looking over the numbers and saying: "Oops. I must have been mistaken. Thanks so much for watching over this money and not misspending it. Sorry to have wrongly accused you," the child shows a complete lack of interest in the bank statement and holds fast to the false belief. The child "knows" that the favored parent is always right, and nothing the accused parent could show him would correct that misperception.

Borrowed Scenarios

If your child is caught up in a loyalty conflict, she may start to make accusations about you that use phrases and ideas borrowed from your ex. It can feel as if you're watching a puppet: your child's mouth is moving, but the words and tone of voice are strikingly reminiscent of your ex. Your child may seem to have been brainwashed or "programmed," employing language and referring to ideas that she doesn't even understand—for example, making accusations that she can't back up or using words that she can't define. An example is the accusation "Grandma is a bad houseguest," a complaint unlikely to have originated with your child, since it's a rare child indeed who cares whether anyone is a good or bad houseguest. Your child may also recall events that never happened or versions of events that put you in a bad light.

In one family of divorce, the mother actually wrote out scripts for the daughter to recite when the father came to visit. The mother reviewed these little plays with the daughter beforehand in order to ensure that the daughter would properly recite her lines. The script usually ended with the daughter screaming at the father that he was a terrible parent and she didn't love him.

In another family, the young daughter came home from school one Friday excited to tell her mother that she had been invited to try the advanced math class. Math had never come easy to this girl, and it was quite an honor for her to be invited to try the class. She explained to her mother that the teacher had assured her that if the class proved too difficult, she could return to the regular math class with no penalty or inconvenience. The next morning, the girl went to spend the weekend with her father. When the subject of the advanced math class came up at the mother's home again on Monday, the girl explained that she had decided against taking the class because, as she explained, "I don't have a track record in math." Nothing the mother said could change the girl's mind. Needless to say, the girl presented her decision as her own and not influenced by her father, who did in fact have a track record—a track record of discouraging his daughter from trying new things and achieving academic success.

Extension of Animosity to Your Friends and Family

If your child is caught up in a loyalty conflict, she may have started to resist spending time not only with you, but also with people in your circle of friends and family. Formerly beloved grandparents, aunts, uncles, and cousins may suddenly be avoided. Your child may deny ever having been close or having fun with them, saying things like "I never really loved Grandma." Your child may not only avoid them but may also denigrate them with cruel nicknames or rude comments. Your child would rather stay with your ex and clean the garage for the weekend than go on a vacation with your side of the family!

As with the other signs of being caught up in a loyalty conflict, this one is also atypical of children who have been abused. In fact, many children who have been removed from their home due to abuse are placed in the care of an extended family member of the abusive parent.

Exercise 2.2: Is Your Child Exhibiting These Signs?

Place a check mark in the corresponding column to indicate how frequently (since the divorce) your child shows signs of the behaviors that we have discussed. If you're co-parenting more than one child, you may want to complete this exercise separately for each child. You can download or print additional copies at http://www.newharbinger.com/29583.

	Never That I'm Aware Of	**Sometimes**	**Often**
A campaign of denigration			
Weak, frivolous, and absurd reasons for rejecting you			

Lack of ambivalence toward you and your ex			
Absence of guilt for bad behavior toward you			
Reflexive support for your ex in parental conflicts			
The "independent thinker" phenomenon			
Use of borrowed scenarios			
Extension of animosity to your friends and family			

If your child is showing any of these eight signs, no doubt you have your hands full. You're probably pretty distressed to feel your child slipping away from you, seemingly impervious to your love, your efforts to correct misperceptions, and your attempts to function as a parent. It's possible that you have tried various strategies and are unsure whether they have been or will be effective. The remainder of the book will present a lot of ideas for dealing with these behaviors that you may not have tried yet. These ideas have worked for others co-parenting with a toxic ex. First, however, we will highlight some common parenting mistakes in this situation.

Common Mistakes When Co-parenting with a Toxic Ex

Following are four common mistakes that co-parents dealing with a toxic ex make: giving in to anger, giving in to depression and defeat, focusing on the wrong thing, and blaming the ex/failure to look at oneself. We'll touch on these mistakes as they relate to specific problems in later chapters.

Giving in to Anger

In an infamous voice message that went public in 2007, actor Alec Baldwin angrily scolded his eleven-year-old daughter for not having her phone turned on to receive his calls. (As of the writing of this book, you can still listen to it on YouTube—search for "Alec Baldwin voice mail to daughter.") While no one condones what he did, it's certainly understandable that parents whose efforts to communicate with their children are blocked at every turn would become angry and frustrated. Of course, we don't know what exactly occurred between Baldwin and his daughter, but his behavior provides an excellent example of a common mistake: taking your anger and frustration out on your child. The key message from research on children who are caught up in a loyalty conflict between their parents is that while outwardly they may behave rudely, disrespectfully, and hurtfully, inwardly they're being torn apart (Baker 2007). To take out your anger and frustration on your child is to confuse the message with the messenger—your child, who's also a victim in this family drama. When you respond to your child in anger, it only serves to reinforce the poisonous messages your child is hearing about you. In this way, you're contributing to your child's rejection of you and increasing the likelihood that your child will side with your ex.

Giving in to Depression and Defeat

A father called me (Amy) one day to discuss his concerns about his young daughter being caught up in a loyalty conflict between him and his ex. His daughter had come for a visit on Saturday morning and excitedly told him about a new art project that she and her mother had worked on the night before: they had made a monthly calendar for the rest of the year. She explained that the days she was going to be home with Mommy were decorated with glitter, rainbows, and unicorns to indicate sunshine and happiness. "And what about the days you'll be with me?" he asked her. "Oh," she said, "they were left blank." At this point in the telling of the story, the father started to cry. He said that he felt sad and demoralized after his daughter shared this story; he said that he felt blank, as blank as the days on the calendar. In fact, he confessed that, as much as he loved his daughter and cherished their time together, he had been unable to rally himself for the rest of their visit. Now he was overcome with feelings of despair and regret. As the conversation progressed, it became clear that the father had allowed the story of the mother trying to erase him to become a self-fulfilling prophecy. His lack of energy and attention to his daughter showed the child that Mommy was right: time with Daddy is a blank. In this way, he unwittingly increased his daughter's distance from and disappointment in him.

Focusing on the Wrong Thing

Some parents, when faced with an accusatory child, will rush to prove that the child is incorrect. To be yelled at and accused of theft (or a similar misdeed) by your child is certainly unsettling, and it's understandable to want to convince an emotionally wound-up child that he has nothing to be upset about. But providing proof of your innocence is usually not sufficient, and that means that your child isn't really upset about the facts at hand. The mistake is to assume that you can rationally explain to your child his error and that to do so strenuously will be more effective. What children typically respond to in this situation is the way in which the parent behaves, not the facts being presented. When you're frantically explaining your innocence or screaming "I'm not a bad parent!" your child doesn't think: *Oh, I see my mistake now. I came to the wrong conclusion.* Instead, he's thinking: *This person is acting crazy, and I don't like it. I want to get out of here—the sooner the better.* The better alternative, which is less likely to contribute to your child's negative feelings and in that way further the conflict, is to address the feeling behind the accusation.

Blaming the Ex, Or Failure to Look at Oneself

Yet another problem is having a hair-trigger reaction to anything remotely problematic that your ex does or says. Having learned about all the behaviors that may induce a loyalty conflict, you may be acutely sensitive to ways in which your ex is interfering with and undermining your relationship with your child, and you may incorrectly assume that every complaint and every suggestion is part of a master plan to erase you. This is counterproductive with respect to your relationship with your child, because it means that you may ignore realistic and constructive criticism, and your child will perceive you to care more about being right or not giving in to your ex than about being an open and truly dedicated parent. It may seem like asking a lot to treat each complaint and criticism with an open mind, even when it comes from a child who has been grossly unfair to you or from an ex who has tried to turn your child against you—but that's what you need to do in order to avoid closing your mind and your heart to self-improvement for the sake of your child.

Conclusion

As award-winning journalist Melinda Blau noted almost twenty years ago, "co-parenting is not for the selfish or immature" (1993, 301). We agree with Blau; yet some co-parents *are* selfish and immature, and generic advice on "how to get along with your ex" will be insufficient if your ex is maliciously undermining you and interfering in your relationship with your child. While it may be helpful, general co-parenting advice by itself—keep your emotions in check, act in an even-handed and businesslike manner, and so on—isn't going to protect your child from loyalty conflicts involving you and your ex. Your first and foremost concern must be how to respond to your ex's manipulation of your child in a way that doesn't further entrench your child's alignment with your ex.

Throughout the rest of this book, you'll learn techniques and strategies to help you respond to your child in a way that empowers you to protect him from the effects of a loyalty conflict and allows him—as much as possible—to love and be loved by both parents.

3

Core Concepts of Positive Parenting

Your goal, as a co-parent with a toxic ex, is to deepen and strengthen your bond with your child so that your child is less susceptible to your ex's attempts to interfere with and undermine your relationship. Positive parenting infused with mindfulness can help you achieve that goal. In this chapter and the next, you'll learn about positive parenting and mindfulness concepts in general. In chapters 5 through 9, we'll show you how to apply these concepts specifically when your child is experiencing a loyalty conflict.

The term "positive parenting" refers to beliefs and skills that help parents have a warmer and more peaceful relationship with their children (Adler 1927; Dreikurs 1991; Gordon 1970; Nelson 2006; Popkin 2002). Core concepts of positive parenting include achieving a balanced parenting style, instilling respect, fostering critical-thinking skills in your child, avoiding power struggles, fostering responsibility in your child, identifying "ownership" of problems, having appropriate expectations of your child, encouraging your child, demonstrating appreciation of your child, and being self-aware.

We'll also present some concepts related to mindful parenting that can be helpful when your child is experiencing a loyalty conflict. "Mindfulness" is the term used to describe an awareness and a way of thinking about awareness of yourself and the present moment, which can heighten your awareness of your own thoughts and feelings and deepen your connection to the people around you. Mindfulness is the "awareness that emerges through paying attention, on purpose, in the present moment, and nonjudgmentally to the unfolding of experience moment by moment" (Kabat-Zinn 2003, 145). The term comes from the Buddhist practice of mindful meditation and can be applied to parenting through a conscious awareness of yourself as you live your life and interact on a moment-to-moment basis with your child (Kabat-Zinn and Kabat-Zinn 1997).

Woven together, positive parenting and mindful parenting provide you with the specific tools and frame of mind to help you strengthen, protect, and heal your relationship with your child who is experiencing a loyalty conflict. With only a few exceptions, the concepts and tips are applicable to children from toddlers to teenagers.

It's helpful to remember that parenting is an active process that's most effective when you're self-aware and when you consciously make parenting decisions based on a rational appraisal process and a loving heart. Parenting requires effort, and your parenting repertoire will evolve over time as both you and your child mature and develop.

Achieving a Balanced Parenting Style

Developmental and clinical psychologist Diana Baumrind (1966) identified three styles of parenting, which reflect different ways to balance parental power (the setting and enforcement of discipline and limits) with parental responsiveness (warmth, affection, and attention to the child's needs):

- *Authoritarian parenting,* in which parents hold high expectations for their children and convey these expectations in a manner that may be perceived as rigid, demanding, and even cold

- *Permissive parenting,* in which there are few demands and expectations for the child's behavior, coupled with high responsiveness to the child's needs
- *Authoritative parenting,* characterized by both high expectations and high responsiveness

Authoritative parents are warm and attentive but firm. They're responsive to their children's needs without being indulgent. This style of parenting is associated with closer, warmer relationships and more responsible children (Baumrind 1966). An authoritative parenting style can help you avoid some of the more obvious parenting mistakes, such as being too lenient or too harsh. It can be challenging to cultivate this style of parenting while your ex is undermining your authority, and you may be tempted to overreact and come down too hard on your child or, conversely, give up altogether out of a sense of defeat or a desperate attempt to avoid conflict. The strategies presented throughout this book can help you achieve the balance that you seek.

Instilling Respect

Respect is a cornerstone of mindfulness and positive parenting, something which ideally works both ways. We recommend that you speak to your child in a kind and respectful (albeit firm, when necessary) tone that conveys deep love and appreciation (even to an alienated child behaving in a problematic manner), and expect and encourage her to speak to you in a respectful manner in return.

You may find it difficult to expect respect from your child, especially if he's already showing signs of being on a campaign of denigration, the hallmark of which is a rude and contemptuous attitude toward you. It may also be challenging to respect your child when you know he's being manipulated and misled. It's important that you learn ways to respectfully set limits and problem solve so that you can model respect and avoid inflaming the conflict with your own anger and harshness.

Tips: Conveying Respect

At times when the two of you are not engaged in conflict, ask your child for his opinion and acknowledge his unique point of view. Let him know that you respect his ideas and feelings, even though you might not always agree.

Use a respectful tone of voice when speaking to your child, even when you're in disagreement.

Don't assume that everything your child says is a coached statement prompted by your ex. Respectfully consider each criticism and complaint.

Use the word "respect" in conversation with your child in order to highlight this aspect of your parenting approach.

Fostering Critical-Thinking Skills in Your Child

Too often, parents overdo the role of teacher, answering all their children's questions proudly as the all-knowing adult. Your child may ask why he has to follow your rules—or go to school, or take vitamins and so on—and it might be tempting to answer with an exposition on the importance of family rules, or going to school, or taking vitamins, and so forth. You could point out the many reasons to follow rules, and no doubt your child would benefit from your wisdom. More importantly, however, when your child asks a question, he's providing you with an opportunity to help him develop critical-thinking skills, or the ability to know his own truth and figure things out for himself. Imagine for example how empowering it would feel for your child if, in response to his question, you said: "Awesome question! What do *you* think? Why *should* you have to follow rules (or go to school, or take vitamins, etc.)?" No doubt your child could—with some encouragement—come up with the same list of reasons as you, but in coming up with it himself he'll feel both pride in himself and appreciation of you for allowing him to demonstrate his intelligence.

If your child is being exposed to the loyalty-conflict-inducing behaviors described in the previous chapter, she's being encouraged to abdicate her critical-thinking skills. One way you can help rectify that is to foster and strengthen these skills in everyday situations, in hopes that she'll eventually apply them more widely in her life, even perhaps to the loyalty conflict involving you and your ex.

Tips: Fostering Critical-Thinking Skills

When your child makes a statement, ask him gently and lovingly how he knows that to be true. Encourage him to look at the source of his beliefs.

When your child makes a statement, ask him whether he might be misled about that. Share a time when you were misled (but use an example that steers clear of parent-child issues).

When watching a commercial together, casually point out how it's designed to make you want something that you may not need.

Point out situations in which your child and a friend may have different perceptions or responses to a book or movie and that just because his friend liked something doesn't mean that your child will. He has his own truth.

At the supermarket, point out to your child how the packaging and displays are designed to lure you into buying things you don't want or need.

Avoiding Power Struggles

Too often, when children exhibit behaviors that their parents want to change or correct, the parents think that they need to exert power and control over the children if they want to correct the behavior. Sometimes you may feel that you must either wage a battle to impose your will on your child or else let your child "get away with" undesirable behavior. Your child, of course, wants to feel in control of her own behaviors and is likely to resist being told what to do. Daily life becomes a struggle for control over the smallest things, because neither you nor your child wants to relinquish any power. Yet it doesn't have to be this way.

Positive and mindful parenting involves finding solutions that don't involve a loss of power and control for the parent *or* the child. The key to avoiding power struggles can be found in many of the specific strategies outlined in the next chapter (offering choices, finding solutions together, identifying family rules, etc.), but you can infuse all your parenting interactions with this principle. The goal of positive parenting isn't to impose your ego and power on your child but to respect your child's integrity as a separate person. When you avoid conflicts—or, when they're unavoidable, you resolve them in a manner that works for everyone—you and your child will feel more warmly toward each other.

This is key, because your ex may be encouraging and instigating conflict between you and your child at almost every turn. You'll need to master the skills and strategies for avoiding unnecessary conflicts and working through those that you can't avoid in a manner that preserves your relationship with your child.

Fostering Responsibility in Your Child

A primary goal of positive parenting is to—over time—make parental authority obsolete. As your child matures and develops, she should be gaining the skills, the attitude, and the desire to be a responsible and self-sufficient person. Positive parenting uses a number of strategies to help children develop those skills and attitudes so that they can make healthy and respectful choices that will allow them to succeed in life.

As a co-parent with a toxic ex, you can help your child assume responsibility for her choices and help her develop the inner strength necessary to resist the pressure to choose one parent and reject the other. To foster responsibility in children is essential for parenting in general and for co-parenting with a toxic ex in particular.

Identifying "Ownership" of Problems

Too often, parents react to every problem their children have as if it were theirs too, even when it's not. It can be freeing for you to realize that your child doesn't need you to intervene in every problem situation she confronts in life. Unless she asks for your input (for example, "Why didn't my friend invite me to her party?"), you don't need to do or say anything if your child appears upset other than show concern and be available to listen if she wants to talk. When your child already has taken ownership of a problem, your intervention could actually prove detrimental to the development of her autonomy.

Sometimes it may be difficult to know when your child's problem isn't yours. Before you react to a problem situation, it might be helpful to quietly reflect on the meaning of the problem for you and try to understand whose problem it is. For example, if your child doesn't do his homework or eat his dinner, whose problem is that? The answer depends on whether you can live with the consequence. For example, if your child skips homework and gets a poor mark or is reprimanded by his teacher, he may learn more from that experience than from you nagging him. Likewise, if your child doesn't eat his dinner, he may learn from the experience of being hungry. If in either of these situations you rescue your child, write a note to the teacher, for instance, or whip up a late-night snack—your child won't learn anything other than that you're available on a moment's notice to bail him out of challenging situations. If you're sarcastic or unsympathetic ("That's what you get for being lazy!"), your child may come to think that you're not on his side, and perhaps will develop the idea that people in general aren't trustworthy. All parents need to figure out how to manage the gray areas in which a problem could be either theirs or their children's, depending on their values and culture.

Discussing "ownership" of problems calmly and clearly will allow you to support your child in a way that lets her know that you trust and respect her as she works through her own problems, and it'll help you be self-aware and articulate why certain behaviors or attitudes on the part of your child pose a problem for you as the caring and responsible adult: they affect your child's health and safety, perhaps, or they cause you unnecessary inconvenience.

Having Appropriate Expectations of Your Child

All parents maintain expectations for their children's behaviors—regarding keeping their room clean, using proper manners, respecting other people's property, and so forth. Even the most permissive parents must have some expectations for their children—children need to get dressed in the morning, eat breakfast, go to school, follow the basic rules of the school—or else they couldn't get through the day As children get older, their parents' expectations usually increase, based on the parents' knowledge of their children and general understanding of child development. Inappropriate expectations on the part of either the parent or the child can result in frustration, anger, and conflict. Positive parenting emphasizes having appropriate expectations and using that knowledge to incrementally increase children's responsibility so that over time they enjoy greater privileges and freedoms. In this way, they'll be ready for life as independent and self-sufficient adults. Parents who do too much or too little for their children can interfere with that process.

Consulting with experts on child development can make it less likely that, as a co-parent with a toxic ex, you'll make a fundamental parenting mistake (like expecting too much or too little in a way that harms or demeans your child) that could harm your relationship with your child and/or be used against you by your ex. Using family meetings and mutual problem solving (see the next chapter) to develop expectations of your child and decide on responsibilities can also reduce conflict.

Encouraging Your Child

Parents who engage in mindful and positive parenting believe in their children and convey to them an attitude of encouragement and faith in their ability to solve their own problems, identify good solutions, and achieve their goals. By seeing the best in your child and encouraging her to try new things, you can help her thrive. Encouragement also involves helping your child develop a sense of her own goals and values so that she's not unnecessarily dependent on others.

You can use encouragement to increase the warmth in your relationship and show your child that he's respected, valued, and trusted, which all children want and appreciate. You can also show enthusiasm for your child's hopes and dreams and encourage him to pursue them. The more your child takes ownership of his own goals and plans, the more he'll hold onto them, and the less your ex will be able to undermine them.

Demonstrating Appreciation of Your Child

Each child is unique, with a combination of appealing characteristics that endear them to their parents and not-so-appealing characteristics that create parenting challenges. Children who are "easy" in one sense (not picky eaters, quick to laugh) may be not so easy in another (prone to illness, moody). Each child has a unique set of talents and skills. A commonality among most children is the need to be understood and appreciated for their individual personality and traits. Appreciation is most beneficial to children when it's specific and when it's shared in a loving manner.

Try to appreciate your child for who he is in the here and now, not for who you want or hope him to be. This appreciation can deepen the bond you have with your child as he blossoms with your love and acknowledgement despite his negative attributes while in the throes of a loyalty conflict.

Tips: Conveying Appreciation

At a quiet moment, reflect on your child and think of her many specific talents and gifts. Then, when you want to show your child that you appreciate her, point out unique and specific aspects of her personality or talents in a loving and warm manner. Let her know that you see her, that you love her for who she is, and that you "get" her.

You can also show appreciation for specific things that your child does that make your life easier or that you respect and admire. Let her know your appreciation by being specific about what she did and how it made you feel.

Being Self-Aware, and Taking Care of Yourself

Mindful and positive parenting requires awareness of yourself, coupled with an acknowledgment of the imperfections of the world and thus your own imperfections. While you might feel that it's a sign of weakness to apologize to your child for making a mistake, in reality it's a sign of strength and commitment to the relationship.

A theme throughout this book is that no parent is perfect. If you can say to your child, "I may have acted rashly just then; I would like to try a different way to share my thoughts about this with you," you'll earn your child's appreciation and respect. A parent who pretends that he's never wrong will create resentment in his child, who eventually will learn that everyone is wrong sometimes (and that pretending infallibility is a way of taking unfair advantage of a child). There's much to be gained from looking at yourself to identify areas for improvement, which you can't do if you need to see yourself as perfect or assume that every time your child complains or criticizes you she's been manipulated by your ex. When you model the ability to apologize and ask for forgiveness, your child may learn by your example.

Self-awareness also means knowing when you're too stressed to make good parenting choices—that you're reacting automatically as opposed to acting consciously—and asking for a "time-out" for yourself. It's sometimes acceptable (if not necessary) to say to your child: "I'm feeling stressed right now and preoccupied with making dinner. Let's set aside some time later to discuss this issue. You're so important to me, and I want to give you my full attention." Doing so can help you prevent residual bad feelings in your child, because you have cleared the air with a sincere apology and your child knows that she's valued and respected. Otherwise, bad feelings may fester, which can in turn make your child susceptible to manipulation by your ex, who will—as noted earlier—pounce on any mistakes you make.

Another aspect of self-awareness is being able to examine the images that you carry in your head. As you go about co-parenting your child who's experiencing a loyalty conflict, explore those images and thoughts to make sure that they aren't reinforcing your sense of impotence, worthlessness, shame, or isolation. One co-parent with a toxic ex shared how she felt like a pathetic puppy chasing after her son, looking for "scraps" of affection and acknowledgment. This image magnified the difficulty of the situation and led her to want to give up in defeat and despair. It may be necessary to actively negate those messages and cultivate more positive ones in order to continue the heroic task of co-parenting with a toxic ex.

Having Compassion for Yourself and Your Child

A key concept in midful parenting is having compassion, which means empathizing with others' suffering and trying to alleviate their pain. Suffering doesn't have to involve a catastrophic illness or major setback—it can refer to the everyday frustrations and disappointments that we all experience when our lives don't unfold as we had hoped. Compassion not only has the potential to improve your relationships but also feels good. Psychologist Alfred Adler is said to have advised depressed clients to do something nice for someone else in order to improve their own mood and outlook (Nelson 2006). *Self*-compassion entails acceptance of your imperfections while striving to improve yourself. Having self-compassion means refraining from self-deprecating and defeatist attitudes that undermine your satisfaction and pleasure.

As a co-parent with a toxic ex, try to always respond to your child with compassion and empathy. This will allow you to maintain feelings of closeness even when you're stressed and under duress—something that is especially important when your child falsely accuses you of some misdeed. Rather than responding defensively and angrily (like "That's not true! I didn't…"), which will most likely create additional ill will, your first response should be to try to understand how your child must be feeling in that moment. The *feeling* of the interaction is what will linger in your child's heart when all is said and done.

Conclusion

You can use a positive and mindful parenting philosophy to strengthen your relationship with your child and limit your ex's negative influence. As a co-parent with a toxic ex, you don't have the luxury of parenting in a reflexive, automatic manner. Try to be mindful of your parenting choices and approach your child—even one who's caught up in a loyalty conflict—with love, respect, and compassion. Your open heart can guide you to choose and implement the parenting and disciplinary strategies described in the next chapter.

4

Deepening Your Bond and Reducing Conflict with Your Child

In this chapter, you'll learn parenting strategies that will help you deepen your relationship with your child, and you'll learn disciplinary strategies that will help you approach and work through conflict in a way that preserves that relationship. Starting in chapter 5, we'll apply the topics covered in this and the previous chapter to co-parenting with a toxic ex. With only a few exceptions, our advice is appropriate to children of all ages.

Parenting Strategies

Parenting strategies that will enhance your relationship with your child include keeping the door to communication open, active listening, nondirective play, praise and encouragement, emotion coaching, training, inviting cooperation, offering choices, and family meetings.

Keeping the Door to Communication Open

Parents and children spend a lot of time communicating with each other. How that conversation feels plays a significant role in children's experience of their parents. Unfortunately, some parents may respond to their children in ways that can interfere with their children feeling heard, understood, and valued.

Fourteen Communication Roadblocks

When you respond in one of the following ways to your child, you create a "communication roadblock" (Gordon 1970) because you're not truly present and listening to your child, trying to understand what he's thinking and feeling. The examples we give pertain to a theoretical situation in which your child comes home from your ex's house angry and making baseless accusations.

1. **Commanding:** "You need to wipe that nasty look off your face right now."
2. **Warning, admonishing, threatening:** "If you throw your backpack in the living room again, I'm going to take it away from you."
3. **Moralizing:** "That's what you get when you let other people boss you around. You shouldn't let your father influence you in this way."
4. **Advising:** "Why don't you just tell your father to stop lying about me?"
5. **Lecturing:** "Children need to learn how to be nice."
6. **Judging, criticizing, blaming:** "You're acting really nasty, and I don't like it one bit. If you let other people tell you what to think and feel, you're going to have a rough time in this life."
7. **Praising:** "You're usually such a nice boy."
8. **Name calling, shaming:** "You're being a bad boy, and I don't like you right now."

9. **Interpreting, diagnosing, psychologizing:** "The problem with you is that you're so gullible. Are you really going to believe every lie your father tells you about me?"
10. **Placating:** "It's not so bad. You'll feel better tomorrow."
11. **Interrogating:** "What did you do now?"
12. **Distracting:** "Let's not dwell on whatever is upsetting you. Let's play a game."
13. **Sarcasm:** "Wow, you have it *so* bad."
14. **Know-it-all:** "The solution is so easy. You just need to change your attitude."

Exercise 4.1: How Communication Roadblocks Feel

Imagine that you're talking on the phone with a friend. You share with this friend that you're having a rough time with your ex and that you're concerned that he's trying to turn your child against you. Now imagine that in response this friend uses one of the communication blockers listed above.

- Commanding: "You have to stop letting your ex control you this way."
- Warning, admonishing, threatening: "If you keep letting your ex upset you this way, I'm going to start to think that you just want to wallow in your misery. I'm really sick of hearing about this."
- Moralizing: "This is what you get when you get a divorce. What did you expect would happen?"
- Advising: "What you need to do is just get a new lawyer and take your ex back to court. Show him who's boss!"
- Lecturing: "When I was going through my divorce, what I found was most helpful was to..."
- Judging, criticizing, blaming: "If you hadn't married that idiot, you wouldn't be in this situation. It's your own fault."

- Praising: "You're such a good mother that your child will never turn against you. You have nothing to worry about."
- Name calling, shaming: "You're such a coward. Why don't you just put your foot down once and for all and stop letting your ex walk all over you?"
- Interpreting, diagnosing, psychologizing: "You obviously have issues with your parents that are clouding your judgment. You really need to see my therapist to work on that. Nothing is going to get better until then."
- Placating: "You'll feel better after a good night's sleep. Everything always feels better in the morning."
- Interrogating: "What did you say when your ex called? Why did you agree to his request? When did he say he would bring your child home? What exactly was the plan that you agreed to?"
- Distracting: "Let's go see a movie and get some ice cream. You'll feel better then."
- Sarcasm: "Well, *that* sounds like the *worst* thing I ever heard."
- Know it all: "First you have to ditch your attorney and develop a new legal strategy, and then you really need to take my advice and..."

How does that feel for you? Would you want to share your thoughts and feelings with this friend again? Write your reflections in the following space (or in a journal or notebook).

____

____

____

____

____

____

Sometimes when your child shares a concern or problem with you—or simply throws his backpack down in frustration and anger and waits for you to ask what's wrong—he doesn't want you to solve the problem for him or tell him what to think, feel, and do. He mostly needs you to care, listen, and be present, so that he feels heard and understood. As we mentioned in the previous chapter, parents don't need to solve every problem for their children, and knowing this should reduce your likelihood of creating communication roadblocks. Instead, you can use mindful and active listening.

Active Listening

Active listening is a mindfulness technique for truly being present as a listener, aiming to not just hear the words but understand what a speaker is saying. Sometimes when your child says something to you that presents a problem—for your child or for you—you might find that rather than paying deep attention to what your child is saying, you're thinking about what you're going to say in response. In this way, you miss an opportunity to truly understand your child and show her that you care about her and her feelings. Furthermore, when your child shares a problem with you, you might make assumptions about what your child is feeling and about what's really going on, based on your own fears or needs. Unless you check the accuracy of your assumptions with your child—through active listening techniques—you won't really understand what's bothering her, and she'll ultimately feel misunderstood and frustrated. For example, you might assume that your child is angry when she's really hurt, or you might assume that the most troubling aspect of a situation is one thing when it's really another.

Mindful active listening involves paying focused attention to the speaker without imposing judgment. It also involves the following six components.

Six Components of Active Listening

1. **Indicating deep attention with nonverbal cues:** Nod your head, make eye contact, and show a relaxed body posture to signal that you're giving the speaker your full attention.
2. **Using words and phrases to show listening and caring:** Make brief verbalizations, such as "I see" and "Go on," in order to show the speaker that you're actively engaged in hearing.
3. **Restating what the speaker has said, to ensure accurate understanding:** Check with the speaker to ensure that you understand what he's saying.
4. **Probing for more information:** Ask questions to make sure you have the whole story—for example, "What happened next?"
5. **Listening for the feelings:** Make an educated guess as to what the speaker is feeling in order to fully understand the experience from the speaker's point of view.
6. **Offering to problem solve:** Encourage the speaker to identify his own solutions, and offer assistance with that process. This doesn't involve telling the speaker what to do or how to (or how not to) think or feel.

Practice active listening with a friend or coworker first, to get a feel for it. At first, it might seem unnatural. Once you feel comfortable with it, try using it with your child. Most importantly, practice "being present" with your child, focusing as much as possible on what your child is saying, what she's feeling, and how she understands her reality, her experiences, her hopes, and her dreams.

Nondirective Attention

"Nondirective attention" is the term used to describe a particular type of parent-child interaction. There are two essential ingredients: paying exclusive attention to your child (don't answer the telephone, check e-mail, make dinner, etc.) and following your child's lead without correcting, directing, or influencing the activity, other than to ensure safety. To start practicing nondirective attention, set aside a specific period of time to spend with your child, and let your child know that you won't be engaged in any other activities during this time. Give your child the opportunity to select the activity, then give him the benefit of your undivided attention without correction or direction of any sort. Your task is to reflect appreciation of your child and his choices and decisions.

When you engage in nondirective attention, you're as fully present as possible, but your child runs the show. For example, if your child selects drawing as the activity and decides to draw in a nonrealistic or technically incorrect manner, don't correct your child's technique. Instead, notice his choice by making a neutral comment, such as "I see." If your child selects playing with a toy farm set as the activity and puts the cow in the chicken coop, don't correct him verbally or place the cow in the barn; instead, say: "You're placing the cow over there. I see." This sounds simpler than it is, because as a parent you're probably used to assuming a teaching role and using opportunities like these to instruct your child about how the world works. It isn't easy to be actively engaged and paying attention but not actively influencing. However, if you can, try to show your child nondirective attention for even a little while every day. It may help to draw on mindfulness activities, such as deep breathing and noticing your attention. If you find your mind wandering, gently bring your attention back to your child, without being overly critical of yourself for letting your mind drift away, and notice your child in the here and now.

Praise and Encouragement

Children of all ages need attention. They would prefer positive attention in the form of hugs, smiles, and the words "I love you," but they will behave in an aversive manner (being disobedient, rude, or arrogant) to attract your negative attention (reprimanding, scolding, and so forth) if that seems to be the only way to receive attention at all. When you give your child enough positive attention, you make it less likely that he'll provoke conflict as an attention-getting strategy. In general, positive attention will deepen the love and connection between you and your child.

Praise is an important form of positive attention. The Center for the Improvement of Child Caring has identified seven elements that increase the impact of praise and its benefit to children.

Seven Elements of Praise

1. **Look at your child.** Make eye contact with your child so that she knows that you care and are speaking and attending to her.
2. **Move close to your child.** Stop whatever else you're doing and move close to your child. Put yourself on your child's level (e.g., if your child is sitting, sit with your child).
3. **Smile.** Let a warm and positive attitude toward your child show on your face.
4. **Say plenty of nice and specific things.** Notice and comment on what your child is doing that you want to reinforce and commend your child for doing. For example: "Look at how neatly you're working. And I like how you put each marker back in the box once you're finished using it."
5. **Praise your child's behavior, not your child.** Avoid saying "Good girl" or "Good boy," because that implies a judgment about the value and worth of your child.
6. **Be physically affectionate.** Gently touch your child's shoulder or pat her head. Your face, body, and words should all work together to convey your love and appreciation for your child.
7. **Do this immediately. Don't delay!** Praise works best when given at the moment of the behavior rather than after the fact, though after the fact is better than not at all.

Adapted with permission from the Center for the Improvement of Child Caring (2001).

Some professionals make a distinction between praise and encouragement, with advocates of positive parenting preferring encouragement. However, praise comes more easily to some parents and can be a good way to reinforce desired behaviors, so we don't want to discourage you from praising your child. In fact, we suggest that you practice praising your child at least once a day, using the seven elements we just outlined.

At the same time, some parenting experts worry that praise, as an external reward, can dampen the child's inner motivation (e.g., Nelson 2006). Furthermore, they believe that praise is too results oriented ("Good job!") as opposed to process oriented ("Nice effort!"). They propose that children do best when their parents *encourage* them rather than praise them, because encouragement is more likely to instill a true connection to their own values and beliefs. So, rather than praising your child for doing a nice art project, you might want to encourage her by noting how focused she is in her efforts or how pleased *she* seems to be in her work. Encouragement could also involve asking questions and helping your child articulate her own appraisal and satisfaction rather than relying on you as the all-knowing expert to tell your child what's good and what's not. Following are examples of encouragement:

- "Look at your improvement!"
- "That 'A' reflects a lot of hard work."
- "What do you think about your work?"
- "You really seem to enjoy art."
- "Are you feeling proud of yourself?"
- "Look how far you have come."

In addition to praising your child, try to make encouraging remarks throughout the day and see how your child responds.

Emotion Coaching

Children (and adults) experience a range of emotions over the course of a typical day. This may be especially true of children who are involved in a loyalty conflict. However, children aren't born with the ability to recognize their feelings, label them, talk about them, and learn to manage them. They need to learn this skill as they grow, and parents play a key role in that process. "Emotion coaching" is the term used by psychologist John Gottman (1998) to describe ways that parents help their children manage their feelings. Gottman identified the following emotion coaching strategies.

Model ways to label feelings. Any time you're experiencing an emotion yourself (e.g., frustration, disappointment), share that emotion with your child if doing so doesn't burden or frighten her. For example:

- "The train is running late, and I'm worried that we may not get to our appointment on time."
- "That person just cut me off in her car, which was annoying to me."
- "I'm so proud of myself today. I handled a tough situation well, and I feel good about that."

We recommend that you not label your child's feelings until you get the hang of labeling your own and until your child is used to hearing you talk about emotions. You might also want to label the feelings of others, such as characters in books or TV shows. For example:

- "The boy in the story was relieved when he found his toy."
- "She seems afraid that her friend will feel angry with her."

You could also ask your child what she thinks someone else is feeling—for example: "I wonder what the little sister in this story is feeling right now. What do you think?"

Validate your child's feelings. Whenever you become aware that your child is expressing feelings, mention that you see the emotion and that it's okay—whatever it is. Remember, there's no right or wrong when it comes to feelings. A certain response to a feeling may be problematic (like hitting you when he's angry), but the feeling is always okay. So you might say:

- "It's okay to feel _____________ right now."
- "I would be _____________ too if that happened to me."
- "Everyone has his or her own feelings. There's no right or wrong when it comes to feelings."

Encourage your child to identify and label her own feelings. Try not to assume that you know what your child is feeling. Mention that it looks like she's feeling a certain way, but then check to see whether you're right. For example: "You seem sad right now. Is that right?" If you're uncertain and don't want to guess, you can just ask, "What are you feeling right now?"

Model how to cope with emotions. One way to show your child by example that feelings—even strong ones—can be tolerated is to use positive self-talk, which means reminding yourself that you can cope with whatever life throws at you and whatever is bothering you. Although you may usually say such things in your head, you can also say them out loud so that your child can hear how you use self-talk to calm yourself and help yourself cope. You might say out loud in front of your child: "I can do this. I'm worried right now because I really want to do a good job, but I'm going to give it my best shot, and I think that'll be good enough. Either way, I can handle it." You can also use mindful self-soothing techniques, such as breathing deeply, breathing slowly, or just breathing more consciously. This would entail breathing slowly, paying attention to your breath, feeling your breath enter and travel through and leave your body. Pay special attention to the point at which the in-breath becomes the out-breath and the pause in between the two. You can also try meditating to calm yourself and gain clarity. Be aware of times when you have strong emotions, and consider them opportunities to teach your child by example how to manage them.

Encourage your child's efforts to manage her emotions. Notice whenever your child is struggling with a strong emotion, and use praise and encouragement to strengthen her capacity for managing it. Your child may not even be aware that she just coped with emotions in a positive and affirming manner, and may benefit from your pointing it out to her so that she can remind herself about her success the next time she feels overcome with emotion.

Training

Much of what children learn over the course of their childhood they learn through play or observation. However, certain skills need to be deliberately taught. One source of conflict between parents and children is when parents have expectations that exceed their children's levels of skill and knowledge levels. Imagine how frustrating it would be for a child who's expected to get dressed when she doesn't know how to pull a shirt over her head or zip up a zipper. When you ask your child to clean her room or do the laundry, she and you may have different ideas about what that task involves, or she may simply not be able to accomplish what's expected.

In the positive parenting approach, you teach your child how to accomplish the tasks that are and will be expected of her. When you ask your child to do something, make sure that she's capable of accomplishing what you're asking. If she shows that she can't complete the job, break it down into manageable chunks and take the time to train her in how to do each one. You can also teach your child basic tasks as you go about your daily routine. For example, when dressing your young child, you might comment: "First we take off your pajamas and put them in the hamper. What do you think we do next? Right, next we get a clean pair of pants. Where are they kept?" If you do this in a lighthearted manner, your child will be learning and absorbing information without even knowing it. Likewise, with an older child, as you set the table, fold laundry, make a bank deposit, or clean the garage, you can identify the steps involved and demonstrate how to perform them.

As you go about your daily routines with your child, start to incorporate "training for success," as it's sometimes referred to in the positive parenting literature (Nelson 2006), and see how receptive your child is to that process.

Inviting Cooperation

Some children will say no to a command or demand simply because there have already been too many requests of them that day or because they just aren't in the mood to be cooperative. An invitation, on the other hand, may feel entirely different to a child. The next time you would like your child to do something that isn't essential for him to do, try an invitation, such as "Anyone who wants to help set the table, feel free to join me now." Or "I could really use a hand folding the laundry." Use a friendly tone; otherwise it won't feel like an invitation. You might be surprised at what your child is willing to do when invited! Just remember not to invite your child to do something when you really intend or expect your child to do it; in other words, when declining isn't an option. For example, don't invite your child to brush his teeth or to go to bed at bedtime. An invitation under these circumstances would feel—and be—disingenuous or manipulative.

Try inviting your child to do something that she hasn't helped you with before, and remember to keep your tone of voice light and pleasant.

Offering Choices

Another time-honored means of gaining cooperation without a power struggle is to provide your child with reasonable choices so that you're not in the position of having to say no. For example, you could ask your toddler, "Do you want to wear the green shirt or the blue shirt?" rather than asking "Which shirt do you want to wear?"—to which your child might respond by requesting a tank top in the middle of winter. You could ask your teen whether she wants her allowance on a weekly or biweekly basis. Make sure that you can live with either choice, such that you're not asking "Do you want to take a shower?" unless *not* taking a shower is an option. You could ask, "Do you want to take your shower before or after dinner?" as long as you feel that either option is acceptable. If your child still balks, then ask for her input. She might suggest an acceptable alternative that you hadn't thought of. If so, go for it and thank her for coming up with a workable solution.

Family Meetings

Family meetings are a great way to build family cohesion, which can strengthen family bonds and prevent conflict and discord. Family meetings aren't just casual gatherings or impromptu discussions. A family meeting has a predetermined time, location, and agenda and follows a specific format. The purpose of the meeting is for all members of your household (not your ex, who lives in another house) to make joint decisions—where to go on family vacation, which charity to support, how to make sure that chores are being done on time—or to identify problems, like dishes being left around the house, or bedtime being ignored, and solve them; as well as to develop cohesion, perhaps by creating a family motto or playing a game. Obviously, certain decisions (i.e., ones that are vital for individual or family integrity) should be made solely by parents, but many other decisions that are typically made solely by parents can be made with contributions from everyone. Note that the purpose of your family meetings shouldn't be to resolve hostility and conflict with your ex but to create cohesion in your own household.

Five Components of Successful Family Meetings

1. **Regular meeting time and location:** Together, the family should decide on a time and place for family meetings, and everyone should commit to being available for every meeting unless there's an emergency.
2. **Ground rules:** Together, the family should decide on some ground rules, such as the following, for family meetings.
   - Only one person speaks at a time.
   - No changing decisions outside of meetings.
   - Treat everyone with respect.
   - No problem is too small for discussion.
   - No idea is too ridiculous to put on the list.
   - No one deserves to be mocked or ridiculed for their comments.

   Write these rules down, and keep them in a place where everyone can easily refer to them at the beginning of each meeting.
3. **Rotating responsibility:** At each meeting, one family member should act as chairperson (i.e., run the meeting) and one family member should act as secretary (i.e., take notes). Everyone, even young children, can have a turn assuming these roles, in order to ensure that meetings are run in a democratic fashion.
4. **Making decisions by consensus:** When discussing problems (chores not getting done, disagreements regarding bedtime, and so on), everyone should have a turn to offer suggestions. Every suggestion should be written down without being discussed until everyone runs out of ideas. Once all ideas are on the table, hold a discussion until a solution is found that feels acceptable to everyone.
5. **End with a fun activity:** The meeting should end with something fun (like a board game, an ice cream party, the development of a family motto) in order to ensure that there are good feelings all around and increase the sense of family cohesion.

Disciplinary Strategies

The parenting strategies we have described should reduce the amount of conflict between you and your child, but probably won't eliminate conflict entirely. You can use positive discipline strategies to resolve conflicts as they arise.

Redirection

When your child is doing something that you want him to stop doing, the first technique to use is redirection. Rather than saying no, simply draw your child's attention to an alternative activity. This works best with young children. Children past a certain age will be too focused on the object or task at hand to easily be drawn to an alternative. When that happens, try a polite request.

Polite Requests

Some children engage in undesirable behaviors innocently—that is, not to be difficult, but simply because of a lapse in memory or judgment. When your child is tired and forgets to put her dirty clothes in the hamper, or when she's excited about a field trip and doesn't put her breakfast dishes in the sink, try quietly and calmly reminding her of what she's supposed to do. This strategy involves awareness of your own emotional state, in order to avoid reacting automatically. The first time you remind her about something, use a neutral tone—don't show anger or make a disapproving face. Show faith that your child will improve her behavior, rather than demonstrating the assumption that she's being purposefully defiant or naughty. A quiet "Please put your clothes in the laundry basket" or "Please remember to put your dishes in the sink" may be all that you need to engender the desired response. Children often rise to the challenge when parents believe in them and see the best in them, and your child is likely to quickly adjust her behavior when spoken to in this way.

If your child doesn't respond after one or two polite requests, try one of the following techniques.

Time-Out and Time-In

While positive parenting prefers the use of "time-ins," which we'll describe shortly, it's important that you understand what a time-out is, in order to make the best use of it. Time-out refers to a period of isolation to help your child cool down and regain control over herself. The key to effective use of time-outs as a disciplinary strategy is to always first give your child a clear message that what she's doing needs to stop or change—and that if she chooses not to stop or change, then she's choosing a time-out. When you do implement a time-out, it's very important that your manner be calm and controlled. If you lose your cool, then you have done no good to yourself or your child. If you feel that you're about to explode with stress or anger, give *yourself* a time-out—tell your child that you need to take a moment to calm yourself because you're feeling tense and aren't sure that you're truly modeling self-control.

When you're calm, collected, and ready to implement a time-out for your child, the rule of thumb is that it should equal your child's age in minutes (*you* decide when it's over, not your child), and as soon as it's over, your child remedies the problem behavior. For example, if you asked your child to stop hitting his brother and he refused to stop, when the time-out is over you still need to address with your child that he was hitting his brother, by having him apologize or at least talk about what was bothering him. Time-outs are best for younger children, perhaps up to about eight years of age. Older children will find it too humiliating. An alternative for older children is to offer them the choice of changing their behavior or removing themselves from the area (for instance, "If you can't stop roughhousing, please take it outside").

An alternative approach is to offer your child a "time-in." Consider that when your child misbehaves, it means he must be feeling badly. Rather than banishing him to another room for a time-out, a time-in gives him special time with you to help him express and release his feelings and regain his composure. While skeptics might argue that rewarding a child with a time-in when he behaves badly would reinforce the bad behavior and make it more likely to occur in the future, experience shows that when a child has his emotional needs met he generally behaves better and doesn't need to misbehave to get attention. At the end of the time-in—just as with a time-out—your child still must address the original problem.

Consequences

The consequences to your child of ignoring a request by you or disregarding a family rule fall into two categories: natural and logical. Natural consequences are the *direct* results of your child's behavior, and logical consequences are those things that you *make* happen. If your child doesn't study for a test, failing the test would be a natural consequence. In other words, you didn't make your child fail the test in order to teach her a lesson. On the other hand, losing her video game or cell phone privileges for a week as a punishment for not studying would be a logical consequence.

In most cases, it's preferable to have your child learn through natural consequences, or from his own experience. Be careful, however, to take a *neutral* stance toward natural consequences when they occur. If you say "I told you so" or "That's what you get when you…," you dramatically decrease the likelihood that your child will learn anything other than that you're not particularly empathetic. Your best response is either to say nothing or to empathize with your child about the tough spot he's in and console him that things will probably work out better next time. Here are some (more) examples of natural consequences:

- If your child dawdles at bedtime, there won't be enough time to read a book before bed.
- If your child is rude, you won't be in the mood to play with her.

- If your child isn't behaving in a safe manner in the car—unbuckling her seat belt, or sticking her hand out the window—you'll have to pull over and wait for her to behave in a safe manner, which could result in missing an activity that you had planned together.

These examples border on logical consequences, because they involve you doing something as opposed to strictly letting nature take its course, but you can still present them as natural consequences rather than as choices on your part.

When the natural consequences of a problem behavior might not be timely or appropriate, you may decide to impose a logical consequence to try to shape your child's behavior. For example, if your child doesn't brush his teeth, he may get cavities—a natural consequence—but it'll take months or years for that to happen. It's doubtful that you want to wait that long for your child to learn the importance of dental hygiene. In addition, some behaviors result in natural consequences so dire (like getting burned by playing with matches, or sustaining an injury by riding in a car without a seat belt) that you can't allow your child to risk experiencing them. Whatever logical consequence you decide on should reflect the "four Rs" (Nelson 2006): related, reasonable, revealed, and respectful.

Related

If the consequence isn't related to the problem behavior, your child may take the punishment too personally. Thus, the more closely the consequence is related to the behavior, the better. Furthermore, because your purpose in imposing this consequence is to teach your child, not to crush his spirit, you should explain clearly the link between the behavior and the consequence and encourage him to do the right thing in future. For example: "I asked you to put your toys away, and you didn't do it, so I'm going to put the toys away for a while, and you can have a chance to play with them again later today. Hopefully, next time you'll be able to put them away when I ask you. I bet you can do it."

Reasonable

The consequence shouldn't be onerous or out of proportion to the behavior. If your child overuses her cell phone, a reasonable logical consequence would be to take it away for an hour, not a week. A week is more than what's necessary to create a teaching moment, and such onerous or extreme consequences tend to increase resentment and negative behavior in children.

Revealed

To "reveal" a consequence means to make it known in advance, to have warned your child about its possibility before you enact it, so that it doesn't feel as if it were imposed out of anger or spite. This is ideal but not always possible.

Respectful

Explain the consequence in a loving and kind manner, not a sarcastic, cold, or demeaning one. If you make your child feel too badly about his behavior, he won't have faith in himself that he can improve. If he feels that you're out to get him, he won't want to rise to the challenge of pleasing you and doing better next time.

Mutual Problem Solving

As a co-parent, when you're in conflict with your child, it can feel like a tug-of-war, with you on one side and your child (and your ex) on the other. Your primary goal in these conflicts is to come to a resolution that works and feels good for you and your child—a win-win. But as important as the outcome is, the process by which you arrive at it is equally meaningful. Say your child wants a ten-dollar increase in her allowance, while you think a four-dollar increase is fair. But you concede to ten dollars by saying: "I'm too tired to keep fighting with you. I give in. You can have the stupid ten dollars. I hope you're happy." Your child will have "won" the money. but lost a feeling of closeness that could have been obtained through warmth and a fair negotiation. Perhaps every time you give your child her allowance, there'll be a residual trace of the bad feeling that accompanied the decision to increase it. On the other hand, if you and your child come to an agreeable solution in a pleasant and respectful manner, every time you hand over the allowance, your child will (hopefully) remember how respectfully the issue was resolved. As a co-parent with a toxic ex, you have all the more reason to avoid resolving conflicts in a way that creates lingering bad feelings.

The key to positive conflict resolution is to start with the "magic we." As soon as you realize that you and your child aren't in agreement about something, say to him: "It looks like we have a disagreement. You want X and I'm thinking that Y would make more sense. How do you think we can work this out in a way that feels good for both of us?" The more you use the word "we," the more you convey to your child that the two of you are on the same team, that you share a goal, and that you can work together to reach a desired outcome.

I-Messages

An "I-message" is a statement about something that's bothering you in which you clearly and directly explain the behavior that you don't like, how the behavior makes you feel, and what you would like to see changed. It's called an I-message because you as the speaker take ownership of your feelings rather than blaming or denigrating the other person. For example, rather than saying to your child, "How many times do I have to tell you to make your bed? You're really not listening to me!" you say: "I feel frustrated when I see that your bed isn't made before breakfast, which means we might be late getting you to school. Can you please make your bed before coming down for breakfast, as we agreed?" In this way, you're stating your feelings rather than calling your child names, blaming him, putting him down, or making him feel badly. You're explaining what the problem is, and you're being clear about what you want to see happen in the future. Furthermore, use of an I-message might result in a discussion that reveals that the problem is your child's and not yours (see chapter 3), that you haven't come to a mutually agreed-upon decision, or that you haven't communicated to him and trained him to achieve what you want him to accomplish.

For the following exercise, think about one behavior of your child's that you would like to improve. Indicate which disciplinary strategies you have tried so far and which new ones you would like to try.

Exercise 4.2: A Behavior You Would Like to Improve

If you're co-parenting more than one child, you may want to complete this exercise separately for each child. You can download or print additional copies at http://www.newharbinger.com/29583.

In the following space or in a journal or notebook, describe one of your child's behaviors that you would like to modify. When does this behavior tend to occur? What do you want to achieve? Do you want to reduce the behavior, eliminate the behavior, or replace the behavior with a different behavior?

____

____

____

Describe the actions you have taken so far regarding this behavior. What has worked, and what hasn't?

____

____

____

Describe at least one natural consequence and at least one logical consequence that might help modify this behavior, and develop a plan for implementing one or the other.

Now, try this plan for at least two weeks. After two weeks, how much improvement has there been?

If you don't see any improvement, it might be because the expectation is unrealistic or because you didn't implement the disciplinary strategy with the necessary love and respect. (Remember the "four Rs.") Try discussing the problem at a family meeting to see whether there's agreement about the problem and to identify new approaches.

Conclusion

Positive parenting—especially when informed by and infused with mindfulness—is both a philosophy and a set of strategies for deepening your connection with your child and respectfully resolving conflicts together as they arise. When you resolve conflicts with clarity and respect, you strengthen the feelings of understanding and care between you and your child. The stronger the bond of love between you and your child, the less susceptible your child will be to your ex's undermining and interference. In the next five chapters, we'll explore how to use these strategies to respond to a child who's being pulled into a loyalty conflict. We recommend that you read these chapters in order, but you can also start with the problem that seems most pressing to you.

Even if you follow all the suggestions in this book, it may not alter the path of alienation and loyalty conflict that your child is on. But that doesn't mean that there's no point in optimizing your parenting and responding strategically. Our suggestions are designed to accomplish the following:

- Slow down your child's movement away from you so that perhaps she'll stay in a relationship with you for months or years longer than she might otherwise, allowing you additional precious time with your child
- Allow you to feel and believe that you did the best possible job and contributed as little as possible to your child's suffering
- Increase the likelihood that your child will return to you one day should she eventually become alienated

5

When Your Ex Is Sending Poisonous Messages About You

As we mentioned in chapter 2, your ex may say things about you to your child that cause your child to feel hurt and angry with you. In this chapter, you'll learn how poisonous messages from your ex can undermine your child's sense of safety and security with you, and how you can use positive and mindful parenting in order to respond to your child's provocations with compassion and empathy.

The topic of poisonous messages is presented as the first of the five sets of loyalty conflict behaviors because each of the other loyalty conflict behaviors discussed in this book is built upon the foundation of the poisonous message. They work in tandem with poisonous messages to confirm, solidify, and validate the messages that your child is receiving about you. In other words, if your ex is sending your child poisonous messages about you, you're definitely at risk of losing your child.

The Effects of Poisonous Messages About You

Even parents who are happily married say negative things about their spouse from time to time. The truth is that co-parenting a child can be difficult. No two parents—even when they're in love—will agree with each other's choices 100 percent of the time. However, as long as their relationship is mostly positive, parents who are married usually won't make negative comments to or in front of their children when their spouse does something with which they disagree.

Once the marriage is over, however, parents have far less incentive to bite their tongues. When there's no longer a marriage to preserve, there's less apparent reason for former spouses to hold back when the other is late, is careless, or simply does something annoying. While it's not great to express negativity like this in front of the children, if it's infrequent and balanced out by positive statements, it won't cause lasting damage. It becomes a problem when one co-parent is overcome with the kinds of feelings described in chapter 1, like anger, jealousy, shame, or hurt, and begins to denigrate the other to such an extent that it places the child at risk of rejecting that parent. If your ex is bad-mouthing you and convincing your child that you're a bad parent and damaged person, then you're co-parenting with a toxic ex. If so, you have an ex who finds fault with every aspect of your personality and conveys disdain to your child through his words, attitudes, and actions. The two essential elements of this behavior are:

- A steady stream of negativity about you
- An absence of any positive messages about you

Poisonous messages are a constant refrain to your child that you're an unworthy if not contemptible person who has no redeeming qualities. Your ex who's sending poisonous messages finds fault with virtually *every* aspect of your personality and characteristics; everything is fair game and is likely to be criticized and picked over for critique. Your ex may criticize your hair, your clothes, your choice of hobbies, your profession, your friends, your family, your cooking, your driving, your taste in movies and music, and so forth. It's all fodder for criticism, contempt, and ridicule.

If you examine the content of the negative messages, it usually boils down to some combination of the following: you're *un*safe, *un*loving, and *un*available. For example, if you get a speeding ticket, your ex may portray you as a reckless driver who's likely to get your child into an auto accident. If you're a mediocre cook, you may be described as someone who can't be bothered to produce a decent meal for your child. If you arrive ten minutes late for pickup or drop-off, your ex may say that you obviously don't love your child enough to come on time. If you arrive ten minutes early, he may say that you're inconsiderate and unloving for rushing your child. This last example shows that there's a negative way to view almost anything you do, such that pursuing time with your child is viewed as harassment and giving your child space is viewed as abandonment. If your ex is determined to turn your child against you, everything you do can—and probably will—be put in a negative light.

There are certain issues related to divorce—for example, finances, adultery, or who moved out of the marital home and why—that children can easily be misled about. Poisonous messages centering on these issues can be particularly damaging. One way that your ex might craft a poisonous message is by conflating the end of the marriage with the end of your love for your child. "Daddy divorced *us*" is a common example, as is "Mommy didn't love us enough to stay married. I guess she just doesn't care about us anymore." Because children can't understand all the factors in adults' decisions, they can easily be misled about your intentions and the meaning of the things you have done.

You may believe that as long as there's little (if any) truth to the statements being made, your child will know that you're a devoted, loving, and involved parent. Your friends and family may reinforce this idea by declaring that your children will be able to discern the truth no matter what. As kind, reassuring, and intuitive as this advice is, if your child is being exposed to negative messages about you—regardless of how little truth is in them—he may eventually absorb them and begin to treat you as someone unworthy of love.

With poisonous messages, it's not just *what's* said but *how* it's said that matters. Some toxic co-parents display strong emotions and are able to convey conviction and believability when making these kinds of statements, appearing sincerely distraught over the other parent's flaws. Children who are exposed to these dramatic displays of emotion may come to believe the content of the messages and conclude that the other parent really is unfit and unworthy. Children generally tend to believe what their parents tell them, even if what's being said is that the other parent is no good. As one child of divorce proclaimed (as an adult) about his mother's bad-mouthing his father: "Of course I believed her. To me she was God!" If your ex is making negative statements about you, they'll carry weight for your child, because your ex is an authority figure and your child will assume that she's telling him the truth. Moreover, mere repetition of a false statement is often enough to trick children into believing it, and if your ex is clever enough to wrap the lie around a grain of truth (an actual event or an actual characteristic of yours), then it'll be even easier for your child to believe it.

And, of course, no parent is perfect, so there's usually a grain of truth to at least some of the criticisms. Your ex will usually be able to find *some* actual fault or apparent weakness of yours to focus your child's attention on and complain about. Over the years, we have seen toxic co-parents whip up their children with such righteous indignation toward the other parent for getting remarried that they declare, "My (mother/father) loves me too much to marry a stranger." Conversely, some toxic co-parents who remarry teach their children to have scorn for the other parent if still single for not having "a life" and being too pathetic to find someone to love him.

If your ex is bad-mouthing you to your child and sending poisonous messages about you, you need to be alert and concerned. This isn't a time to rest on your laurels and assume that your child will know what's what and who's who and therefore be immune to manipulation and deceit. You need to be on guard, not at ease. You need to be thinking strategically about what to do. Children *can* be fooled. They *can* make bad decisions. They *can* be easily persuaded. Research on suggestibility, for example, demonstrates that adults can implant false memories in children (Ceci and Bruck 1993).

Simply repeating a question about an event that never occurred may lead a child to report remembering that supposed event. Later, despite being told that the event never took place, the child will adamantly cling to the false memory. Even adults can be persuaded to believe that something happened when it didn't, as shown by research psychologist Elizabeth Loftus (1997). What this means for you, as a co-parent with a toxic ex, is that having the truth on your side isn't necessarily enough to protect your relationship with your child.

Is This Happening in Your Family?

You probably notice how your ex treats you and speaks to you in front of your child at transition times, when you call on the phone, and at events that both of you attend. If your ex rolls his eyes when you speak, makes your phone calls seem like intrusions, or makes negative comments about your actions, appearance, or beliefs in front of your child, then you know with certainty that your child is receiving poisonous messages about you.

Perhaps you have virtually no contact with your ex and hence no opportunity to observe what he says and implies about you. In some families of divorce, all transfers take place at the child's school, and the two parents rarely come into contact with each other. If this is your situation, then it's not likely that you'll be able to witness what messages your ex is sending about you. It's also possible that your ex knows better than to reveal his denigration of you and is on good behavior when you're around. There are, however, other ways to determine whether your ex is denigrating you and poisoning your child against you. For example, if your child says the following kinds of things to you, you can conclude with great certainty that there's bad-mouthing and denigration going on.

- "Mommy says she loves me too much to start a new family."
- "Daddy's right—you are stingy."

- "Daddy told me that you drive too fast and I need to tell you to slow down."
- "Mommy said I can call her if I feel unsafe with you."

Especially indicative are statements your child makes that use "borrowed scenarios": words and phrases that are unusual for your child because the concepts are too advanced or outside her frame of reference (see chapter 2). Obviously, if people in your circle of acquaintances begin to tell you that your ex is denigrating you, this is an indicator of poisonous messages; and your ex's statements about you in court or in court documents are also illustrative of his views of you. Although these statements may not necessarily be repeated verbatim to your child, at a minimum they reflect the types of things that your ex might be saying.

Exercise 5.1: What Poisonous Messages Is Your Ex Sending to Your Child?

In the first column of the following table, write something your ex or your child has said or done that shows that your ex may be sending your child poisonous messages about you. In the second column, write what you think the message is in each case. If you're co-parenting more than one child, you may want to complete this exercise separately for each child. You can download or print additional copies at http://www.newharbinger.com/29583.

Specific Incident That Indicates That Your Child Is Getting Poisonous Messages About You	**Poisonous Message**
Example: *I overheard my ex tell my child I don't feed him enough.*	*I don't love my child.*

Common Responses That Do More Harm Than Good

If your ex is bad-mouthing you to your child, there are three major land mines for you to avoid:

- Trying to convince your child that she has been misled and/or manipulated (focusing on the wrong thing)
- Responding to your child with anger, frustration, sarcasm, or harsh and unnecessary punishment (giving in to anger)
- Treating every concern your child expresses as though it comes from your ex, not your child (blaming the ex, failing to look at oneself)

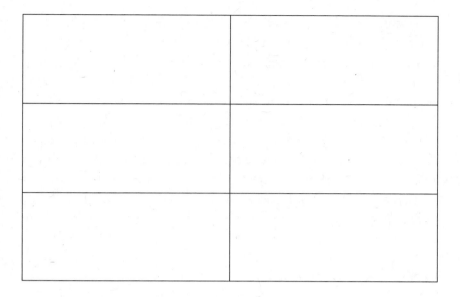

First, just because you believe that your child is caught up in a loyalty conflict doesn't mean that you can simply explain this truth and all will be right again in your relationship. Unfortunately, once an idea takes hold inside a child's mind, it feels like a personal truth based on the child's own experiences. Moreover, if you try to tell your child that his perceptions are incorrect, he'll probably be offended. "Who are you to tell me what I'm thinking and feeling?" is a likely response. Likewise, it's not easy to convince a child that a memory isn't real; and to do so would be insulting, unless done with the proper attention to the child's emotional state.

If you bluntly and perhaps angrily tell your child that your ex tricked her into believing something, your child will probably become offended and angry *with you* for suggesting that she can't tell truth from lies, fact from fiction, reality from fantasy. It would be the rare child indeed who would respond by saying: "Thanks for explaining to me that I've been wrong about all of this. I appreciate knowing that." More likely, your child will "shoot the messenger." Thus, despite being certain that your child is being deceived, exploited, and manipulated, you can't simply deliver that message to your child and expect it to result in a resolution of her divided loyalties. Most likely, it will backfire and further entrench her false beliefs and hostility. Something more is required.

Second, don't take the bait that your ex has laid out for you. When you get angry at your child for insulting your integrity—for example, if he accuses you of misspending child support money—you're likely to use the communication roadblocks described in chapter 4, such as "How dare you accuse me? Have you been sneaking into my files?" (interrogating), "How dare you talk to me that way?" (warning), or "You're being brainwashed against me" (psychologizing). There's very little likelihood that these responses will help repair the damage being done to your relationship with your child. In fact, they'll most likely increase your child's disaffection for and alienation from you. What your child will remember about these interactions is the negative feeling he has from being with you (e.g., "Dad's right—Mom really is crazy," "Mom's right—Dad is out of control and angry"), and what will be lost is the content you're trying to communicate ("Mom made some valid points when she showed me the asset distribution list" or "I'm really glad that Dad explained the pension plan allocations"). Your child will remember *how* you spoke, not *what* you said.

Third, avoid being so defensive that you dismiss every complaint your child has about you as nothing more than a "borrowed scenario" implanted by your ex. Doing so may result in your dismissing legitimate complaints or requests. When you stop hearing your child and only hear your ex's hatred for you, you miss opportunities to empathically connect with your child and improve your relationship. Even if you're convinced that there's absolutely no truth to a specific complaint that your child is expressing, it's a mistake to act on that assumption in a way that closes the door on your child's expression of his thoughts and feelings.

Exercise 5.2: Poisonous Messages in Your Relationship with Your Child

Reflect on the feelings that arise when your child accuses you of something that you believe reflects a poisonous message. What's your typical response, and how well does it seem to work? Write your thoughts in the following space, or in a journal or notebook. Doing this should help you understand how your emotions may be getting in the way of good responses to poisonous messages about you. This will help you begin to develop more effective strategies. If you're co-parenting more than one child, you may want to complete this exercise separately for each child. You can download or print additional copies at http://www.newharbinger.com/29583.

How I usually feel when my child says or does something that reflects one of my ex's poisonous messages:

____

____

What I usually do in response, and how helpful it is on a scale of 1 to 10:

____

____

Suggested Responses

In this section, we explain and illustrate ways to respond to evidence that your child is receiving poisonous messages about you using the parenting and disciplinary strategies presented in chapter 3 and 4.

Active Listening

Children who are exposed to poisonous messages about one of their parents may come to denigrate that parent, resist visitation, and exhibit all the signs of being caught up in a loyalty conflict (see chapter 2). If your child has come to believe (at least in part) some of the negative messages about you, she'll respond to you in a distorted manner based on false beliefs. Such children can be difficult to parent, because they may behave in a hostile, disobedient, and disrespectful manner. Your challenge is to respond in a way that *enhances* your relationship with your child rather than exacerbates the negativity and conflict. Important here is the use of active listening, which involves trying to understand the experience from your child's perspective.

It may be difficult when your child is attacking you and accusing you of being a bad person, an inadequate parent, and someone to be denigrated and possibly discarded, but no matter what your child accuses you of, your first response must be one of empathy and compassion. Put aside your hurt in order to understand whatever *feeling* your child is expressing. Most likely that feeling is hurt or anger. Before your mind races through all the reasons why your child is mistaken and you try to correct the misunderstanding, pay attention to your child's emotional state. This doesn't mean letting your child scream in your face or do anything equally disrespectful. But it does mean not allowing yourself to be distracted from your child by thoughts about how you have been wronged or maligned.

Tips: Responding to Disrespect

It may be difficult to avoid using communication roadblocks when you feel as if you're under attack, such as when your child complains about you or your parenting. You may also need to try very hard to keep yourself from becoming defensive.

Following are examples of things you can say to help you keep an open heart and a cool head when your child who's receiving poisonous messages about you expresses a concern about or criticism of you in a disrespectful manner.

- "I love you too much to let you talk to me that way."
- "It's hard for me to understand you when you talk in that tone of voice. Can you say it again in a calmer tone of voice, so that I can really hear what you're saying?"
- "It hurts my feelings (and my ears) when you speak to me in that tone of voice. Can you say it again in a quieter voice? Because I would like to understand what you're thinking and feeling."
- "It's hard for me to process what you're saying, because you're yelling at me and glaring at me. If you can find a more respectful way to share your feelings, please do so. Maybe you need some time to cool off before we talk about this again. I care about your feelings and want to hear what's going on with you."
- "If you're going to scream at me, I'm not going to stay in the room. You'll have to calm down before we can continue the conversation. I see how mad you are, and I want to understand your feelings, so I hope that we can talk this through."

Following is an example of what could happen if you use communication roadblocks with your child who's attacking or accusing you. Next is a different version of the same dialogue, illustrating the use of compassion, empathy, active listening, and staying focused and in the moment.

Version 1

Daughter: How dare you steal my child support money? Daddy told me what you did, and now he has to work extra hard to make more money because you're so selfish. I hate you!

Mother: (Thinking: *Here we go again. I can't believe that her father has managed to rile her up to make her so upset with me. I haven't done anything wrong. All I did was ask him to show me the bills for the school so that I could see for myself what the tuition is rather than paying him directly. I bet he's been cheating me and is punishing me for trying to hold him accountable by dragging our daughter into this problem. This is so like him!*) Don't talk to me in that tone of voice! I haven't stolen your money, and frankly I don't appreciate you accusing me of doing so. You have no idea how hard I work and how little Daddy gives me. Do you want to see the bank statements? I can show you where the money goes. The judge looked at all of the papers and sided with me. Did you know that? I bet Daddy didn't mention *that* to you!

Daughter: *(Nastily, glaring.)* Dad said that you wrote him a mean letter and now he has to go back to court. All because of you! You're so greedy and mean.

Mother: (Thinking: *I hate when she calls me greedy and mean. It really makes me feel badly, and it reminds me of how* he *used to talk to me in that same tone of voice.*) If your father hadn't lied to me, I wouldn't have had to write that letter. Why don't you ask your father how much he really pays for tuition, and then you'll see who's the thief!

Daughter: Daddy's right. I hate you! *(Storms out of the room.)*

Mother: (Thinking: *I can't do anything right!*)

Version 2

Daughter: How dare you steal my child support money? Daddy told me what you did, and now he has to work extra hard to make more money because you're so selfish. I hate you!

Mother: (Thinking: *She's so upset. Her father probably said something to encourage her to believe that I have hurt her. I haven't done anything wrong, but I must try to stay focused on what she's feeling and what she needs from me right now.*) Dear, you seem so upset right now. I'm wondering whether you're really feeling angry and maybe hurt because you're thinking that I haven't been fair about the money. Can you tell me more about your feelings? I really want to understand what's going on.

Daughter: *(Nastily, glaring)* Dad said that you wrote him a mean letter and now he has to go back to court. All because of you! You're so greedy and mean.

Mother: (Thinking: *I have such a hard time when she calls me greedy and mean. It really makes me feel misunderstood, and it reminds me of how* he *used to talk to me in that same tone of voice. But despite her arrogance, she's really a victim in all of this. I hate to see her so torn apart. What can I do to alleviate her suffering?*) So you think I'm greedy and am doing things that hurt your daddy, and that makes you feel sad maybe? Or angry? Maybe at me? I wonder whether you feel as though I really don't love you or else I wouldn't do these things that you think I did. Can you tell me whether that's what you're feeling? I want to understand what's going on for you.

Daughter: Don't you love me, Mommy? *(Starts sobbing and falls into the mother's arms.)*

Mother: (Thinking: *My poor child. I hate that she has to go through this. I wish that her father and I could get along better, for her sake.*) This isn't easy for you. You're hurting and need to know how much I love you. I do love you—very much. I can assure that you I didn't steal your money, and I want you to know that it's Mommy and Daddy's job to work this out.

The mistake made in the first version is paying attention to the surface issue, money, while ignoring the child's underlying feelings. In the second version, the mother addresses the child's negative feelings head on. She also corrects the misunderstanding, but only after the child shows she's receptive.

One reason that co-parents may be disinclined (if not actually afraid) to talk about their children's feelings—especially negative feelings their children have about *them*—is because they're afraid that drawing attention to those negative feelings will give them more momentum and traction. The worry is that if you say to your child, "You seem angry at me," your child will become even angrier and respond, "Yes, in fact I'm *damn* angry!" But usually just the opposite happens. When you gently inquire about your child's feelings—even negative ones—your child feels more loved and nurtured, which helps the negative feelings dissolve. Don't avoid calling attention to your child's hurt and anger; more often than not it's the path toward healing, and you don't need to be a therapist to talk to your child about feelings. The most important thing is to respond to your child authentically, in a safe, loving, and available manner—especially because the point of the poisonous messages that your child is receiving is that you're unsafe, unloving, and unavailable. No matter what your child accuses you of, you must acknowledge your child's feeling and work from there.

Think for a moment about a child who's missing a friend, pines for a lost toy, or is in some other way experiencing a loss. You might worry that to bring it up—to mention the friend or the lost toy—would exacerbate the child's longing because it would remind the child of her loss. But the converse is true: to sensitively discuss the loss with love and care would help the child cope with it. To say, "You seem to really be missing your (friend, toy) right now—is that so?" would provide the child with the understanding she needs in order to process her feelings and move beyond the grief.

It can be particularly challenging to address negative feelings with children who are caught up in a loyalty conflict, because their alienated stance can be so off-putting. Your child may be invalidating you and telling you in multiple ways that you don't matter and have nothing important to say or contribute. It may be daunting to even attempt to bridge the divide by inviting a dialogue about what's troubling her. You might find it helpful to consciously bring to your awareness an image of your loving child who needs and values you, to help you gather the courage to reach out to her in times of conflict.

If you focus only on your child's outward behavior, her cold, harsh, and mean demeanor, it's harder to see that what your child really needs is love and reassurance. In the second version of the preceding dialogue, the mother reminds herself that her child—despite acting like an entitled, nasty, and spoiled child—is really confused and in pain. By drawing her own attention to her child's suffering, she's able to activate her empathy and respond in a loving manner. But note that she also corrects the misunderstanding when the time is right. She does not let the poisonous message go unchallenged.

Sometimes children feel overwhelmed by their feelings and have difficulty remembering that feelings come and go—they don't last forever. One way you can help your child cope when he's consumed with negative feelings is to put those feelings in a time frame. You might say, "You seem so upset right now; hopefully you'll feel better tomorrow," or "This is a tough time, but tough times come and go. Bad feelings don't last forever." This can give your child a vision of a better, less emotionally fraught future.

In summary, the three steps to using active listening when your child is accusing you of something that you didn't do are:

1. Pay attention to feelings, yours and your child's.
2. Remember that your child is suffering, and respond in a compassionate manner.
3. Try to address the specific concern—but only after the feelings have been addressed.

You might want to mention to your child that you're willing to discuss the details of the accusation (if appropriate) once she has calmed down and is feeling better. If it's not appropriate to discuss the details, you might want to say, "Sometimes when moms and dads divorce, they don't always agree about how to share the (money, time, furniture), and if they can't agree, the judge can help them work it out. You don't need to worry about this; that's what the judge is for. But let me reassure you that I have not (insert the specific thing you're being accused of)." The purpose of this statement is to remove your child from the middle of the conflict without bad-mouthing your ex while reassuring your child that you wouldn't hurt her in the way that she's thinking that you have. Avoid statements like "I can't believe your father told you about this. That was really wrong of him." If you can discuss the issue without burdening your child, then offer to do so. For example, if your child claims that you didn't tell your ex about his school play, reassure him that you did, and comment that perhaps you and your ex can improve communication to avoid problems like this in the future. We need to make two critical points here, however. First, discussing the details will be helpful only if your child is receptive. Don't rush to "make your case" until your child's emotional needs have been addressed. Second, don't show your child anything that could be construed as "too much information." Don't confide in your child or divulge legal or financial matters. In general, you shouldn't show your child legal documents like motions or certifications, because doing so could be used against you in court.

A final point about active listening is that it may not result in an immediate thawing of your child's attitude as seen in the sample dialogue above. So don't despair if active listening doesn't seem to work for you, especially the first time you use it. It may be helpful to think about your use of active listening—and all the parenting strategies presented in this book—as a tool to lay the groundwork for a better future for you and your child.

Exercise 5.3: Times When Your Child Did or Said Something That Reflected Your Ex's Poisonous Message

Think about times when it was clear that your child was receiving poisonous messages about you. (You may want to refer to the first two exercises in this chapter.) How did you respond? See whether you can identify ways to improve your responses to enhance and strengthen your relationship with your child. If you're co-parenting more than one child, you may want to complete this exercise separately for each child. You can download or print additional copies at http://www.newharbinger.com/29583.

What Your Child Said or Did	Your Child's Emotions	Your Response to Child's Actions	Was Your Response a Good Fit?	What You Might Do Differently Next Time
Example: *Accused me of stealing his college money*	*Sadness, anger*	*I said that my ex was a liar and got mad at my child for accusing me of something I didn't do.*	*No—I got angry back and we had a big fight.*	*Pay attention to my child's feelings rather than vent my own emotions.*

Seeing Loyalty Conflicts from the Inside Out

Inside every alienated child is a child who feels rejected. This is an essential insight. Whenever your child who's caught up in a loyalty conflict cruelly rejects you, know that he's actually feeling rejected *by* you. This is what, in part, fuels the intense feelings of hostility and anger that your child expresses. Your child has been tricked into believing that you don't love him. The reason that your child has come to believe this is because your toxic ex has manipulated him to misinterpret and overreact to your normal imperfections and flaws. Your ex may also have lied and misled your child into believing things that are entirely false. As stated earlier, there may sometimes be a grain of truth to your child's accusations. The grain of truth helps the lie take hold within your child's heart and mind. Also, children are naturally egocentric—meaning that they assume that they're the cause of events that occur in their life—so they're primed to interpret your actions as reflections of your feelings for them.

Parental behaviors that seem particularly ripe for exploitation by the other parent have to do with issues such as money, remarriage, and moving out of the family home. These are issues that most children of divorce deal with, even in the absence of loyalty conflicts. If your ex is trying to turn your child against you, she may exploit your past behaviors to create the impression that you're unloving and selfish. If you sense that your child has feelings about these issues, proactively discuss them with your child in order to clear some of the confusion and reduce the negativity. Here's some sample language to consider using.

Remarriage: "I wonder whether you feel that because I remarried it means that I'm the one who ended the marriage and that I love your (stepmom/stepdad) more than I love you. When I married your (stepmom/stepdad), it really showed you that there was no chance that (Mommy/Daddy) and I would get back together. Maybe that was a secret wish you had, and now you know that wish can't come true, all because of me. That might make you feel sad or even angry at me. Maybe it looks to you like (Mommy/Daddy) cares more about you and the family than I do because I'm the one who got remarried. I see how it could look that way for you. I want to reassure you that both (Mommy/Daddy) and I love you and we'll both always be your Mommy and Daddy."

Moving out of the marital home: "I wonder whether you're mad at me because I moved out of the house. It might seem to you that I didn't really care about you or maybe that I was trying to get away from you. I'm so sorry if my moving out made you think that I don't love you or want to be with you. Someone had to move out, and (Daddy/Mommy) and I decided that it would be me. We thought that would be best for the family. But I see from your point of view it probably looked like I wanted to get away from you. Nothing could be further from the truth."

Finances: "I'm wondering whether you have concerns about how money is being divided up between (Mommy/Daddy) and me. I know that it could seem as if I'm being unfair or greedy, but I want you to know that (Mommy/Daddy) and I are going to try our best to be fair with each other and make sure that you have what you need. You can let me know if you hear something or if you have a feeling about the money and you want to check with me."

In each case, it's essential to pose your statement in a gentle, questioning manner by starting with "I wonder" so that you're not imposing *your* agenda on your child. Likewise, it's safest to avoid mentioning your ex as being behind your child's thoughts and feelings or suggesting that he or she's responsible for the loyalty conflict. The minute you point your finger at your ex, your child will no longer be able to hear what you're saying; you close the door to further communication. The one exception is if your child voluntarily and with no prompting from you reveals that your ex said something that caused your child to hold these negative thoughts of you, such as "But (Daddy/Mommy) told me that...." Then your response can be something like "I'm sorry that you were brought into the discussion. I want you to know that it's simply not the case that I (stole your money, stopped loving you, etc.), and if (Daddy/Mommy) told you that, then (he/she) must have been quite angry and upset at the time. That happens sometimes with divorce. But please know that I (do love you, didn't steal your money) and that Mommy and Daddy will work this out."

Using Self-Awareness to Protect Your Child

Another parenting technique that you may find helpful is to consider whether there's any truth to what your child is accusing you of and, if so, to sincerely apologize to your child for your share of the problem. You can do this without making yourself a doormat, or suggesting that you agree that you're a terrible person or a total failure as a parent. You can admit your flaws while coming from a place of strength. In doing so, not only will you improve your relationship with your child, but also you model for your child how to gracefully apologize—a valuable life lesson.

When you explore each complaint in a rational and loving manner, you express your love and concern for your child and take advantage of opportunities to connect with him and learn something about your relationship from *his* perspective. Rather than taking the bait that your ex has prepared for you, you're using these moments as relationship-promoting opportunities. Keep an open heart and a cool head when your child expresses a concern about or criticism of you. In fact, consider thanking your child for sharing his criticism, because it'll keep the lines of communication open, offer you opportunities in the future to improve your parenting, and demonstrate to your child that you welcome his feedback.

Self-awareness is also important for being tuned into (and disrupting) automatic thoughts that may lead you to make less than ideal parenting choices when your child pushes your buttons. For example, if your ex is a bully and your child starts to behave in a similarly aggressive manner, you might think *My child's a monster.*

My ex ruined him. I can't and won't take this abuse from my child! Perhaps your parents favored your sibling over you and you grew up feeling inferior and unloved, which could result in certain reflexive responses when your child shows a preference for your ex, your ex being like your sibling in this case. When your child shows a preference for your ex, you might feel embarrassed or ashamed, leading you to think: *I can't do anything right. No matter how hard I try, it's never good enough. What's the point of showing up at my child's soccer game when she'll ignore me as long as her mother is there?* These negative thought patterns are counterproductive and could lead you to lash out at your child in anger or give up your parental role in defeat rather than respond to your child with loving empathy. Finding someone—say, a trusted friend or mental health professional—with whom you can discuss the feelings and thoughts that you experience when your child behaves badly can help you identify and improve your reactions. When you get a "reality check," you can determine what baggage from your relationship with your ex or even childhood is affecting your relationship with your child.

Being the Message

When interacting with your child, try your hardest to always *be* safe, loving, and available. As a co-parent with a toxic ex, you don't have the luxury of being a mediocre parent. You need to spend time engaging in meaningful interactions with your child. You need to invest yourself, your time, and your attention in the relationship to cultivate a deep and abiding bond that will be less susceptible to your ex's interference and attempts to undermine your authority. You also need to be aware of how the things you do and say look and sound to others, because that could be reflected back to your child or work against you in court. For example, if you go around denigrating your ex to other people, if you are or even just appear to be unsafe, or if you're emotionally unavailable to your child, this may be reported to your ex and/or a custody evaluator, and it could hurt your relationship with your child as well as your image as a good parent. If you have a child who's six months away from no longer being legally required to use a booster seat and you let her ride in the car without one, you could be accused of child endangerment. If you leave your ten-year-old alone in the house while you fetch your younger child from a play date down the street, you could be accused of providing insufficient supervision. You must do your absolute best to not cut corners or appear to ignore safety precautions. Ensure that your child arrives at school on time every day with his homework done. Be polite to your child's friends' parents and don't denigrate your ex to them. At all times, be mindful that everything you do can (and may) be used against you in a court of law. You don't have the luxury of bending the rules or putting yourself first. It's much better to be safe, loving, and available than to have to explain to the court (or your ex or your child) why you weren't.

Being Attuned to Your Child's Unique Personality and Needs

Some children are a natural and easy fit with their parents: the way that the parent likes to show love is the way that the child can feel loved; the parent's natural style of play matches the child's natural style of play; the two have similar temperaments, communication styles, and levels of energy. But not all parents and children are naturally simpatico in these ways. An athletic parent might have an artistic child. An extroverted parent might have an introverted child. All parents, but especially those co-parenting with a toxic ex, must be mindful of their children's preferred modes of relating to others and experiencing love in order to ensure that they're giving love in a way that their children will readily be able to receive. Some children really feel loved when they snuggle with their parent at bedtime while reading a book. Some children feel loved when their parent plays pretend with them. For some children, love is best experienced through rough-and-tumble play. It's important for you to really know your child—especially as she matures and changes over time—and to give your child love in ways that feel like love to her, even if that means stretching yourself and expanding your repertoire.

Exercise 5.4: Understanding How Your Child Experiences Love and Closeness

Keep a journal for a week or two, making note of the times when you feel closest to your child and when you sense that your child is feeling closest to you. Pay special attention to the context: what you were doing, where you were, who else was there, and what you believe promoted the feeling of closeness. Then summarize that information in the following chart to arrive at the big picture. If you're co-parenting more than one child, you may want to complete this exercise separately for each child. You can download or print additional copies at http://www.newharbinger.com/29583.

Situations and Activities When Your Child Experiences Love	**Situations and Activities When You Show Love**

You can—and, as a co-parent with a toxic ex, perhaps should—bring to your child's attention when you're having shared loving moments with him. You don't want to be heavy-handed or too obvious by saying something like "Your father says that I'm a bad mother, but see how we're having fun right now?" But it might be possible to comment, when the time is right, on how nice the feeling is between you and your child. When you're having a moment of closeness, you can say, "I'm really enjoying our special time together right now." It may make it harder for your child to believe that he doesn't feel close to you or that you're never loving if you point out moments of closeness to your child as they happen.

Likewise, you can invite your child to share with you ways in which you can improve as a parent, and you can try—within reason—to improve in those ways. You can invite constructive feedback by saying: "No parent is perfect—me included—so if there's any way that you would like me to improve as a parent, feel free to let me know. I love you and want to be the best parent that I can be." This shows you to be open and loving and can help deflect any future criticism that you don't care enough to be a good parent.

Conclusion

If your child is exposed to poisonous messages about you, he may hold false beliefs about you that lead him to respond with misguided attitudes and emotions toward you. Underlying your child's nastiness and arrogance, which result from being manipulated by your ex, is a painful feeling that you don't love him anymore. When you use active listening in response to your child's accusations, you can avoid "taking the bait" and transform the conflict into an opportunity to improve your parenting and deepen your bond with your child.

6

When Your Ex Is Interfering with Contact and Communication

In this chapter, you'll learn about strategies your toxic ex might use to limit both your face-to-face contact with your child and your communication with your child during periods of separation. We'll describe common mistakes for you to avoid if your ex is interfering in your relationship with your child in this way. You'll also learn how to use positive and mindful parenting to strengthen your relationship with your child and deal with an interfering ex. First we'll look at interfering with contact, and then we'll look at interfering with communication.

The Effects of Interfering with Contact

For your toxic ex, interfering with contact with your child can work hand in hand with poisonous messages about you. The way it works is this: First your ex exposes your child to messages that portray you as unsafe, unloving, and unavailable, planting seeds of doubt about your worth as a person and as a parent. Then your ex encroaches on your parenting time, so that you have fewer opportunities to show your child through shared time together that you *are* safe, loving, and available. (Telling your child that you love him is important, but showing him is even more important. You can't convince someone of your love through words alone.) Furthermore, the less time you spend with your child, the fewer opportunities you have to share the small moments of his life with him.

You probably have noticed how children live in the moment. They burst through the door thrilled to have achieved a goal, or come shuffling in dejected to have suffered a disappointment. The parent who has the pleasure of being on the other side of the door when the child comes home from school is the parent who has the opportunity to have a lived and shared experience with that child. It's so much more impactful to have the experience in the moment while the feelings are fresh and present than to hear about it later on the phone or the following day. In addition, the parent who shares the moment with the child has the greatest opportunity to help the child make meaning of the experience. Sharing an experience isn't a passive process in which the parent merely listens and empathizes with the child's emotions. It provides the parent with an opportunity to shape the child's understanding of the experience. For example, parents who aim to promote independence can respond to their children's successes and failures in such a way as to reinforce their sense of responsibility for their choices. For example, a child who does well on a math test can be reminded about the effectiveness of his study habits, and a child who's invited to a birthday party can be taught to value the experience and to appreciate the host for inviting him. Parents are enormously powerful influences on how children understand their world. Almost every experience can be viewed from different perspectives. For example, a child's passing a test can be attributed to the teacher for having explained the material patiently or to the child for having studied diligently. The parent who spends the most time with the child will by definition have more opportunities to shape his or her beliefs, values, and relationships. When your ex deprives you of time with your child, she denies you vital opportunities to play a role in shaping your child's character and personality, let alone his relationship with and understanding of you.

Yet another way to understand the impact of your ex's limiting your time with your child is the less time you spend with your child, the more unusual it will seem to your child to be with you. She'll become used to spending less and less time with you such that visits with you may become annoyances that intrude on her "real life." If your ex desires to steal your child's heart and mind from you, she'll do so by making it inconvenient *for your child* to spend time with you so that eventually it's your child who resists visitation. Your child won't want to go with you because it'll disrupt her routine and involve the loss of continuity in her life. Your child will feel that she has *one* real home and *one* real life and feel that time with you is outside of that home and that life. The more your ex can have your child internalize disaffection for you, the less work she'll have to do in isolating your child from you. Your ex will be able to claim that she *wants* your child to have a relationship with you but simply can't make your child change her mind. While *you'll* know that this isn't the case, it'll appear to others—and, more importantly, to your child—that the desire to resist (if not actually reject) you comes from within your child, rather than being imposed on her by your ex. It'll become that much more difficult for you to enforce visitation, because your child's thoughts and feelings that you're not a valued parent will be harder to change.

Limiting contact, like all the other parental behaviors that may induce a loyalty conflict—sending poisonous messages about you, erasing and replacing, encouraging your child to betray your trust, and undermining your authority—may take many different forms. It might involve coming fifteen minutes early to pick your child up on Saturday morning. It might involve a plan to swap days that's conveniently forgotten when it's your turn to receive the makeup day. Your ex might routinely take you to court to modify the parenting plan—asking for greater and greater time. Some co-parents don't even bother going through the court and simply take their children for additional time. They may have learned that some courts are typically quite lenient with co-parents who fail to follow court orders, especially when the violations are on a small scale—say a day here or there. In one research study, 90 percent of the co-parents who believed that their ex was trying to turn their child against them said that their ex didn't follow the court order and was rarely penalized for it (Baker 2010). In fact, many complained that the court actually rewarded their ex who made "time grabs." For example, if the ex took more parenting time than allowed, and the other parent filed a motion to enforce parenting time in response, the ex then typically filed a cross-motion explaining why the parenting plan should be modified to reflect the "current arrangement." The court, seeming to look favorably on the status quo, often revised the parenting plan to reflect the new schedule, even if the schedule evolved out of a violation of the original parenting plan.

Your child's attitudes and actions, as well as her beliefs and feelings, may become aligned with your ex's in this case, just as in the case of the other behaviors that co-parents use to induce loyalty conflicts. Eventually, your child may appear willing to go along with any changes in the schedule, including ones that make no sense, violate prior understandings and agreements, or are patently unfair. She may be ready for pickup at an earlier time and behave as if that's always been the pickup time. She may fail to see the unfairness of the situations that continually deprive you of your parenting time.

The Effects of Interfering with Communication

Unfortunately, if your ex is trying to turn your child against you, he's not going to foster your communication with your child. Quite the opposite. Your calls to your child's phone may go directly to voice mail, if you're lucky enough to have been given the number in the first place. Your text messages and e-mails may be blocked or go unanswered. Days may go by with virtually no contact between you and your child. In the meantime, your child is having many experiences—good and bad—which you're not even aware of and of which you may never, or only much later, learn.

An important part of this is the lack of reciprocity by your ex. Despite blocking you at almost every turn in your efforts to communicate with your child, your ex will expect to enjoy nearly constant access to your child when he's with you. There's likely to be a steady stream of commentary and dialogue between your ex and your child when your child is with you. In fact, co-parents who want to induce a loyalty conflict are quick to exploit the latest technology to help them maintain ongoing communication with their children. This allows them to function as a filter or screen between their children and the other parent. Thus, for example, rather than having a discussion with *you* while the two of you are in the car, your child may be engaged in a text-message dialogue with your ex. While your child may also frequently text his friends, it can be more intrusive when he texts your ex, especially when your ex is denigrating you; and simply telling him to stop will likely draw criticism from your ex. Cell phones and the Internet provide toxic co-parents with a means to insert themselves into their children's experience of the other parent in "real time." With text and instant messaging, your ex can be right there in the room commenting on your choices, like what you serve for lunch, and inflaming your child's anger or resentment, encouraging him to see the worst in you.

In the world of drama, a "Greek chorus" is a group of people onstage that provides a sort of running commentary on the action. Your ex may function as a kind of Greek chorus in your child's ear, providing a running commentary on you and your relationship. It can be so intrusive that you may feel as if your child is never free from your ex's insidious influence and everything you do is subject to criticism.

Is This Happening in Your Family?

Before you make any assumptions that your ex is interfering with your contact and communication with your child, keep a detailed diary of your parenting time and all revisions to the schedule—planned or unplanned—for at least a month. You can use the next exercise for this purpose (and download additional copies of it from http://www.newharbinger.com/29583) or follow a similar format in a notebook or journal. If your ex proposes any change in the schedule, respond via e-mail so that you have a paper trail. Likewise, put any changes *you* propose in writing. Keep your e-mails cordial, polite, and concise. Remember, they could end up in court as evidence of your attitude and behavior toward your ex.

In some families of divorce, the parenting plan is rarely if ever changed. For example, if one parent's relatives come to visit for a weekend but the children aren't scheduled to be with that parent that weekend, then the children simply don't see the visiting relatives. Similarly, if one parent wants to take the children to a special event, like a show, but it turns out that the event will occur during the other parent's time, then the schedule is similarly respected. In other families, requests for changes and trades are routine. There's nothing inherently good or bad about these different styles, and arguments can be made that both approaches are in the "best interests" of the child. However, it seems clear that when one co-parent is trying to induce a loyalty conflict, requests for changes in the plan tend to favor that parent. That is, if you have a toxic ex, he may make requests for changes that, over time, allow him to have more parenting time than scheduled. Moreover, the requests themselves may be stressful for you if they require a greater degree of contact and communication with your ex than you would like. In your diary, make special note of any requests for changes, who initiated the request, whether the request was objectively fair, and what the consequences are for you and your child.

Gathering evidence of interference with communication will involve keeping track of every time you attempt to contact your child and whether you get through or not. Likewise, try to keep track (unobtrusively) of the amount of communication between your ex and your child while your child is with you. It's important that you not let on what you're doing, because it may be interpreted in a hostile manner. Your child might respond with "Why are you keeping track of how much I talk to (Mommy/Daddy)?"

The goal of keeping a diary of contact and communication is to accumulate pertinent facts. Once you have a clear and objective picture of the pattern of contact and communication, you'll know whether you really have a problem.

Exercise 6.1: Monthly Diary of Your Parenting Time

	Week 1	**Week 2**	**Week 3**	**Week 4**
Number of days/nights I was supposed to have				
Number of days/nights I actually had				
Specific days/nights I did not have				
Reasons why my parenting time was lost (I traded, it was taken, my child refused, etc.)				
Comments/notes on communication				

Common Responses That Do More Harm Than Good

If your ex is encroaching on your parenting time and interfering with your communication with your child, there are three major land mines for you to avoid:

- Giving up on trying to exercise your parenting time (giving in to depression or defeat)
- Failing to make the most of the time you have (focusing on the wrong thing or giving in to depression or anger)
- Confiscating your child's cell phone (giving in to anger)

Co-parents whose parenting time is constantly being encroached on often feel victimized and outsmarted by their ex, who seems to find endless ways of winning. Some co-parents under these circumstances eventually give up. By way of an extreme example, a father who had visitation every Sunday showed up at his ex's house week after week in hopes that his children would be allowed or even want to visit with him. He longed to hear their voices, feel their warmth, and share in their excitement about their daily interests and activities. Every Sunday, he made the long march up his ex's front pathway and knocked on the door. Inside he heard movement and sounds, confirming that someone was in the house. His ex's car was in the driveway. But sometimes no one would answer. Other times, his children came to the door and coldly glared at him, declaring that they weren't going with him and that he should just go away and never bother coming back. Sometimes his ex answered the door and told him that she simply couldn't make the children come to the door. "What am I supposed to do?" she asked. "Carry them to your car kicking and screaming? It's your fault they don't want to be with you. It really isn't my problem, and I wish you would stop blaming me for your poor relationship with the children." As he dejectedly walked back to his car, he thought: *What's the point? Why should I keep doing this? It'll never change.*

If you're sometimes faced with a closed door or the outright refusal of visits, you might similarly say to yourself that there's no point in continuing to try. But you should focus on your goal of preserving your relationship with your child, not on the signals of rejection that you're receiving. Recall that the point of the poisonous messages that your child is being exposed to is to convey to her that you don't really love and cherish her. In that case, to remove yourself from the situation is to confirm that message in the mind of your child. "See?" your ex can say to your child. "I told you that your (mother/father) really doesn't want a relationship with you. If (she/he) did, (she/he) would have shown up this morning." Likewise, if you stop calling or texting, your child may think (if you're the mother): *Dad's right. Mom never calls me; she probably isn't thinking about me or missing me when I'm with Dad.* As we noted earlier, children are egocentric and will likely conclude *Mom doesn't love me.* Later in this chapter, we discuss finding a way to forge ahead despite feelings of shame and defeat.

The second response to avoid is allowing yourself to feel so dejected, deflated, and despondent that during your parenting time you become emotionally flat or detached. As is the case for many co-parents with a toxic ex, sometimes at the start of your parenting time your child will announce some surprising and disturbing turn of events. For example:

- "(Mom/Dad)'s taking me to a psychiatrist so that I can tell him that I don't want to spend time with you anymore."
- (Dad/Mom)'s taking me on vacation for the whole week next week!" (And this happens when next week is your scheduled parenting time and you have made plans that can't be easily changed.)
- "(Mom/Dad) took me to my own lawyer so that I can tell him that I want to live with (her/him) from now on."

What's so shocking about statements like these is that your child is announcing a fait accompli, a final decision about something that you should have been informed about well before a decision was made. To find out about a decision in this way may feel like a slap in the face. You may be stunned, your mind racing to make sense of this information especially as it relates to your parenting time and your relationship with your child. You may desperately feel the need to check in with your attorney or your friends to share and process your grief and fear, but it's vital that you not let your feelings overwhelm you and distract you from being present with your child. Unless it's a legal emergency, say you receive news on a Friday afternoon and need to get in touch with your attorney that day or else—try to put the bad news out of your mind, at least during your parenting time.

Even when the situation isn't as dramatic as the above examples, it can still cause you to become distracted and despondent. Maybe your child makes an offhand comment that denigrates you. Maybe she announces that she's giving up a once beloved hobby, or maybe she's radically changed her appearance since you last saw her. Any of these situations could lead you to lose sight of the fact that your child is right in front of you and that you must try at all costs to not squander the opportunity to connect with her here and now. If your attention wavers, your child might conclude that you really *are* unloving and don't care about her and her needs. On the other hand, sometimes your reaction to bad news and unwelcome developments may be one of anger, frustration, or fear: "What do you mean you're going with your (father/mother) next weekend—don't you remember that we have tickets for the show?" "How could (you/he/she) do this to me? I worked so hard to make those plans." Try to remember that your child is just the messenger and that a negative response will only bring your child further into the conflict, because it puts her in the position of having to defend your ex's decisions, entrenching her alignment with your ex. In this way, the time that you have with your child will be tainted by strife, discord, and acrimony, confirming the poisonous messages your child is receiving about you. At times like this, the land mine to avoid is being so focused on the latest problem—which certainly feels like a crisis—that you lose sight of the fact that your child is right in front of you, providing you with a precious opportunity to deepen your relationship and strengthen your bond with her.

The final land mine to avoid is confiscating your child's cell phone. Cell phone usage is a common battleground for besieged co-parents, who become frustrated at the way in which the phone keeps the child tethered to the other parent. It may be as if your ex is constantly in the room, whispering in your child's ear, inciting conflict and discontent. You may feel as if you can't have a moment alone with your child or ever be free of your ex's intrusion and influence. However, if you take away your child's cell phone rashly rather than as a logical consequence that reflects the "four Rs", it can cause tremendous conflict between you and your child, again confirming in the mind of your child your unworthiness and your ex's apparent singular importance.

Suggested Responses

In this section, we explain and illustrate how to respond to interfering with contact and communication using the parenting strategies presented in chapters 3 and 4.

Being Present: Nondirective and Mindful Attention

Every parent has attention lapses. Some aspects of parenting are difficult or boring, even though you adore and cherish your child. For example, some parents don't enjoy taking part in pretend play and find make-believe tea parties beyond tedious. Other parents don't enjoy athletics and would happily pass on playing catch or watching a wrestling match with their children. When you were married, you could probably have your ex do the things you didn't enjoy, and you likely did the things that your ex didn't enjoy. But now, you probably do a little bit of everything. If you're a single parent, you don't have the luxury of passing on the puppet shows and board games. You have to do it all. It's likely that you'll find your mind wandering while doing activities you generally don't like. Likewise, you'll probably find your mind wandering if your child has just surprised you with some disturbing news—perhaps your ex has a new girlfriend, whom your child has already met and supposedly adores; your ex got a new job and you have concerns about the implications for your child support; or your ex bought your child a puppy, which is likely to entice him to stay with her more than ever.

No matter what, your job as a co-parent with a toxic ex is to be present with your child, setting aside your worries for another time and trying to find ways to be engaged in even the most tedious of tasks. The key is to practice the following mindful parenting techniques, which involve keeping your attention focused on the here and now and being emotionally present in all your interactions with your child.

Making the Most of Every Moment

When you're present and attending to yourself and your child, you can focus on enjoying yourself and find ways to make even the most tedious activities more engaging. If you can let go of your preconceptions, your worries, and your regrets and simply live in the moment, you may find unexpected pleasures. For example, if your mind wanders while you're playing with your child, gently bring your attention back to the play at hand. When you pay attention to the small details of how your child plays, you'll no doubt find things that surprise or delight you. Breathe deeply and fully to relax your mind and body, which can enhance your attention and your pleasure. As in meditation, being mindful of your breath can sometimes help anchor you in the present moment. Remind yourself that feelings like anxiety, fear, boredom will pass—that feelings come and go.

Exercise 6.2: Practicing Mindfulness

Practice mindfulness techniques for the next two weeks and then use the following chart to note which ones you tried and how helpful they were for you on a scale of 0 to 10.

Mindfulness Technique	**How Helpful Was This for You? (0–10)**
Breathing deeply	
Staying relaxed in your body	
Paying attention to yourself and your child	
Allowing the feelings to pass	

Practicing Gratitude

Remind yourself every day of things that make you feel grateful. Even when you're really suffering, you can find solace in a sense of gratitude. Time with your child is surely something to be grateful for, especially if you have a toxic ex, although it may be challenging to feel grateful when your child is behaving rudely and disrespectfully.

Exercise 6.3: Practicing Gratitude

Practice gratitude strategies over the next two weeks and then note in the following chart how helpful they were for you on a scale of 0 to

10. This will allow you to understand which ones are particularly useful in your parenting journey. If you're co-parenting more than one child, you may want to complete this exercise separately for each child. You can download or print additional copies at http://www.newharbinger.com/29583.

Gratitude Technique	**How Helpful Was This for You and Your Child? (0–10)**
Asking your child at mealtime or bedtime to identify something that engenders gratitude	
Noticing times when you're feeling close with your child and experiencing gratitude for those moments	
Noticing other aspects of your life for which you're grateful	

Seeing Challenges as Opportunities

Rather than letting challenges defeat and demoralize you, try to be open to the possibility that what looks like a defeat may hold within it an opportunity. The next time you experience a challenge, use the following exercise to help you learn and grow from it. Ask yourself how and what you can learn from this experience, what your choices are, and how you can live your values and dreams right now.

Exercise 6.4: Learning from Challenges

Download and print complete copies of this exercise at http://www.newharbinger.com/29583. A sample entry is provided here.

Challenging Situation	**What You Can Learn**	**What Opportunity Is Presented**
Example: *My child told me that she loved her stepmother more than she loved me, and I became depressed and lost my focus for the rest of the evening.*	*My feelings of fear that I was losing my daughter overwhelmed me and led me to not be present with her for the rest of our visit.*	*I can see now that I had an opportunity to really listen to her and love her, but my feelings overwhelmed me and I lost my focus. I'll try to use mindfulness techniques to stay focused even when I'm scared or upset.*

Using Positive Self-Talk

The things you say to yourself affect your perceptions and feelings. If you say things that make it seem as if everything is bad and nothing will ever get better, it can actually make it harder for you to function and find solutions. Your thoughts can defeat and paralyze you. For this reason, try to avoid negative self-talk, such as:

- "I can't take this anymore!"
- "This is too hard for me."
- "Nothing I do makes a difference."

These kinds of statements can affect how you feel and behave. When bad things happen to you, try to pay attention to the thoughts running through your head. Listen to what you're saying to yourself. If you find that you're making negative statements, try to stop and remind yourself that you have courage, strength, and resources to help you face challenges. Try to use positive self-talk instead. Complete the following exercise to remind yourself of your strength and courage.

Exercise 6.5: Identifying Your Inner and External Resources

Write your answers to the following questions in the spaces below, or in a journal or notebook.

Describe a time when you did something that you didn't know you could do.

____

____

What inner resources do you have (intelligence, courage, etc.)?

____

____

Which of your friends have been most supportive?

____

____

What external resources do you have—friends, mental health professionals, books?

____

____

Awareness of Yourself

Maintain awareness of your internal states, feelings, and thoughts by checking in with yourself to see how you're feeling and whether you're acting with conscious intent or simply reacting automatically based on your emotions. Several times a day, try to take a moment to see how you're doing and what you're feeling. Be kind to yourself; accept your limits while you strive to continue to meet your parenting goals and values.

Tips: Practicing Self-Awareness

Ask yourself, "How am I doing right now?"

Ask yourself, "Do I need to slow down before I act? Do I need some time for myself?

Remind yourself that you're a work in process. Don't expect perfection.

Find an inspirational poem or saying about self-acceptance, and post it in a place where you'll see it often.

Find a time every day to practice self-acceptance. For example, in the morning before you start the day, remind yourself that you're a good and loving person who deserves respect. Or before you go to bed each night, identify something you did that day that makes you feel especially proud.

Appreciating Your Child's Unique Personality and Characteristics

Pay attention to your child; really try to know her and appreciate her as a growing individual. Understand her specific character and personality, and let her know that you cherish her and that you "get" her for the person she is.

Exercise 6.6: Appreciating Your Child

Write your answers to the following questions in the spaces below, or in a journal or notebook. If you're co-parenting more than one child, you may want to complete this exercise separately for each child. You can download or print additional copies at http://www.newharbinger.com/29583.

What did your child do recently that amazed or surprised you?

____

____

What are your child's special talents and strengths?

____

____

When and how do you show appreciation for your child?

____

____

When you follow these guidelines, it should bring you and your child closer, help minimize the influence of poisonous messages about you, and make up for the encroachment on your parenting time. In addition, you may find it helpful (if not necessary) to bring to your child's attention the good times that you share together, as mentioned in chapter 3. For example, prior to the end of a visit, you can reflect on the best parts of the visit with your child. Share the moments that were meaningful for you, and ask your child to share the highlights from his perspective. Bringing the good times to your child's conscious awareness will make it harder for your ex to rewrite history and erase your child's good memories of you (see chapter 7). In addition to practicing gratitude for the positive aspects of the visit, ask your child whether any aspects of the visit were difficult for him and what might make your time together even better. This will provide you with an opportunity to practice empathy (a key component of mindfulness) with your child.

Some parents may be wary of introducing what could be a negative thought or feeling into a positive moment, but these times are actually the best times to discuss difficulties, because your child is more receptive when he's in a good mood.

Creating Connections While Apart

As a co-parent, you know that you and your child will often spend time away from each other. As one with a toxic ex, you also know that your ex may behave in ways that make it difficult for you to connect with your child during those absences. Your task is to keep your connection with your child alive in ways that don't rely on traditional means of communication, since those are likely to be thwarted. (Nonetheless, you should continue to call, e-mail, and text your child while he's away from you, both in the event that your call is answered and to prevent the accusation that you don't care enough to even bother to reach out.) We hope that the ideas we discuss next will help you get creative.

One idea is to buy a bag of chocolate kisses. First, give a chocolate kiss to your child and say something like "Here's a chocolate kiss. I'm going to pack a few in your bag every now and then, and every time you find one you'll know that I'm giving you a kiss. I think about you all the time when we're apart, and I want you to know that." Then leave one on her pillow one night and put one in her jacket pocket one day, to get her used to the idea of associating the candy with your love. When she leaves for your ex's, put a few chocolate kisses in her backpack or suitcase. When she finds the candy, she'll be reminded that you care and that you're thinking about her. In this way, you *are* communicating while she's away. You can also make or buy little cards with cute pictures and messages of love and put them for your child to find in her backpack, pants pockets, notebooks, and so forth.

A second idea is to say something like this to your child: "Do you see the moon (or sun, or stars) up in the sky? When you look up at the moon and the moon is shining down on you, I want you to know that the same moon is shining down on me as well. And every time you see the moon I want you to know that I love you and am thinking about you and looking forward to when we'll be together again." In this way, you can "communicate" with your child without interference from your ex.

Another way to forge a connection during periods of absence is to take some time during each visit to plan together what you'll do on the next visit. In that way, your child will look forward to being with you again, regardless of your ex's attempts to persuade him otherwise. Even if it's something as simple as baking cookies, seeing a movie, or shopping for school supplies, the plan will be something your child can look forward to, and in that sense he'll be thinking of you while you're apart. For younger children, posting and maintaining a calendar so that you and your child can keep track together of each visit could prove useful. You can use stickers and art supplies to decorate the calendar and create a monument to your shared time. The more your child looks forward to time with you, the more difficult it'll be for your ex to manipulate your child to give that time up. This doesn't mean bribing your child with something good to look forward to each visit; it does mean making a plan together for how you'll spend your special time. When you strengthen your connection with your child in these concrete ways, you leave less room for your child to be negatively influenced and doubt your love.

These kinds of efforts to maintain connection and communication while your child is away are good for any parent-child relationship. But if your ex is trying to turn your child against you, they're *vital*.

Persevering and Taking the Long View

Some co-parents feel overwhelmed by their ex's interference with their contact and communication with their children because of the hostility or the disappointment, and they respond by giving up on their relationship with their children. They stop communicating during periods of absence, and they stop showing up for visits. This is an understandable response to the situation, but one that carries with it many potential disadvantages, the primary one being (as we mentioned) confirmation in the mind of your child of the poisonous message that you don't love her.

Here's one way to think about this situation that may help you persevere. You have so much love for your child and you want so much to be with him that to walk up to your ex's door, knock, wait, and then turn away feels devastating. You're being denied the opportunity to give your child all that you have to give. Or so you think. To you, knocking on the door means nothing if it doesn't result in a visit. But from your child's point of view, your knocking stands as proof that you still love him and still value the relationship. Your knocking—which means so little to you compared to all that you have in your heart to give—means the world to your child, because it represents the difference between nothing and something. If you think about the knocking from your child's perspective, you can recognize its value, importance, and power.

Another reason to forge on—even when your ex intercepts your letters, blocks your calls, and doesn't answer the door—is that if you don't, your child may one day ask you why you stopped writing, calling, and coming to visit. Instead of going into a long diatribe about how your ex prevented you from connecting with her so you stopped trying, which will sound like nothing more than finger-pointing, you can simply say, "I didn't." And it will be the truth, and by the way you say it your child will believe you. Furthermore, when you act forthrightly and from true parental caring and your desire for a relationship with your child, there's always a chance that this effort to stay connected and maintain the relationship will permeate her awareness and help break through the lie that you don't care. Some children have found stashes of letters written to them by their alienated parent, proving that the favored parent blocked attempts at communication. Some children have heard the distant knocking on the door or glimpsed their alienated parent from an upstairs window and realized that they hadn't been forgotten or abandoned after all. It may require the cumulative weight of many little efforts to finally allow your child to see you for who you are: a loving parent who consistently, maybe even heroically, tried to reach her child. Children who were reunited with their parents following a period of alienation have acknowledged the importance of persistence and consistent messages of love (Baker 2007).

If you have no ongoing contact with your child, consider reaching out—if you have the means—to send a message every day or so. Keep the message light and brief, and basically reiterate that you love your child and are available to spend time together.

Tips: Communicating with Your Alienated Child

Don't denigrate or blame your ex. Avoid saying things like "Your (mom/dad) won't let me see you, so I'm writing to say..." If you reconnect, there'll be a time and a place to clarify your ex's role, but until then, your child won't be able to hear this message.

Don't invoke feelings of guilt or try to manipulate your child. Avoid statements that go like this: "If you ever thought about anybody but yourself, you would know..."

Don't show self-pity. Avoid lamenting about how the lack of communication and contact affects you, such as "I ache and miss you so much."

Do invite your child to share his perspective with you so that you can better understand the hurt and anger he's feeling.

Dealing with Cell Phones

Because children's cell phones pose such a problem for co-parents with a toxic ex, they warrant special mention. We strongly suggest that, regardless of how much its use intrudes on your precious parenting time, you avoid confiscating your child's cell phone. We have seen this backfire and become the focus of the "pounce," as described in chapter 2. Your ex will most likely simply purchase your child another phone and refuse to give you the number. Then you'll be in a worse position than before. The more reasoned approach would be to discuss with your child—perhaps using the family meeting format or joint-problem-solving approach, both described in chapter 4—some commonsense rules regarding cell phone use on which everyone can agree, along with consequences for not following these rules. For example, your child's cell phone must remain in the kitchen overnight and not be used during meals and study time or else you'll prohibit its use for a period of time.

Keeping Your Child Out of the Middle

Imagine that your child begins a visit with a news bombshell: "Daddy is moving away and I'm going with him" or "Mommy has decided I should go to school in her town, and I love that school!" In addition to staying calm and focusing your attention on your child, you'll need to employ some basic parenting tools to remove your child from the middle of the parental conflict. It may be tempting to respond to the facts as they're being presented to you: "Where's Daddy moving to, and why didn't he tell me first?" or "What do you mean, you're moving there? What makes you think the schools in your mother's town are so good?" But any response that engages your child in the content of the news will give her the message that it's acceptable for her to be in the middle of a discussion on the topic. As tempting as it might be to ask for details, explanation, or clarification, the only appropriate response is to gently indicate that she has no place in a discussion of the matter.

Tips: Taking Your Child Out of the Middle

Here are some examples of things you can say when you're tempted to respond to your child about news from your ex's house.

- "That's for Mommy and Daddy to discuss."
- "I'll follow up on that with your mother later, but right now let's..."
- "I see. Well, I'll call your father later and find out what's going on."
- "You know, it really isn't your job to pass on this kind of information. If Daddy has something he wants to say to me, he can say it directly, and I'll mention that to him."
- "That sounds interesting, and I certainly want to hear more about that from Mommy. Right now, let's..."

Use a kind and relaxed tone of voice that doesn't convey anger or recrimination. Remember to be aware of your breathing, remind yourself that you have the inner resources and courage to handle the problem, and, most importantly, focus your love and attention on your child in this moment.

Conclusion

If your ex is limiting your parenting time and your opportunities to communicate with your child during periods of separation, your child may come to believe that you don't want to spend time with him and that you don't care enough to call or write. Your child may also become acclimated to spending less and less time with you. In response, you can use mindfulness techniques to pay deep attention to your child, to help you cherish and to enrich the time that you do have together. You can also develop creative ways to communicate your love and maintain a connection with your child during absences. If you no longer have physical access to your child, you can derive inner strength from the knowledge that no matter what, your child needs to know that you love him. You can do your best to find ways to reach your child despite your toxic ex's interference.

7

When Your Ex Is Erasing and Replacing You

In this chapter, you'll learn how your toxic ex might try to erase you from your child's heart and mind and replace you with a substitute parent. Then we'll show you how to respond with positive and mindful parenting when these behaviors affect your child.

The Effects of Erasing and Replacing

There are several specific "erasing and replacing" behaviors. All share a common element of trying to erase you from your child's heart, mind, and memory and install someone else (usually a new paramour or spouse, but sometimes a grandparent) in your place.

Referring to You by First Name

Obviously, if you invite your child to refer to you by your first name or she has done so throughout her life, then it can hardly be viewed as a manipulation by your ex if she continues to call you by your first name following the divorce. But, if you have always preferred "Mom/Mother" or "Dad/Father," and your ex suddenly starts to use your first name when speaking about you to your child, it encourages your child to do the same and may fuel a loyalty conflict.

In most if not all cultures throughout the world, children refer to each of their parents by a special name ("Mommy" or "Daddy," "Mamá" or "Papá," and so on). A child's use of this name is a signal to others that this person is the child's parent—and, as such, has a special relationship with, is responsible for, and has authority over him or her. This name may also be a term of endearment and affection.

If, when speaking to your child, your ex starts to refer to you as "Mary" instead of "Mom," "John" instead of "Dad," or something similar, this is a matter for concern. Your ex is sending your child the following dual message:

- You're no longer a special person in relation to him.
- You no longer have responsibility for or authority over him.

Furthermore, your ex is influencing your child to believe that you're not worthy of respect. When your child refers to you by your first name, it demotes you from parent—someone special and important—to just another person in your child's life. Your child, in essence, is saying: "I don't belong to you. You're not special to me. You have no authority over me." This may feel just as hurtful and demeaning to you as a slap in the face. You may feel ashamed, depressed, or defeated, or you may become angry and resentful.

Installing a Replacement

If your ex has a new partner or spouse, your ex may start to refer to *that* person as "Mom" or "Dad" instead of you, not only to your child but to your child's teachers, coaches, friends' parents, and so forth. One child said of her new stepmother, "When I call Sue 'Sue,' she says, 'What?' [in a cold and clipped tone of voice], but when I call her 'Mom,' she says 'What, dear?' [in a warm and loving tone]." This child was being encouraged, by use of emotional rewards, to refer to her father's new wife as "Mom." In one family of divorce, the children wore not their own last name but that of their mother's new boyfriend on their hockey jerseys. During their hockey games, the boyfriend would cheer them on, calling them by *his* last name. In this way, he was showing the community that he—and not their father—had the more important and enduring relationship with them. It's not hard to imagine how humiliating that was for the father.

When your child refers to your ex's partner as "Mom" or "Dad," you may feel ashamed, as well as angry with both your ex and your child. You may also find yourself in some awkward situations. For example, if your child's teachers and coaches have already been introduced to *your ex's partner* as your child's mother or father, they may respond with surprise when they eventually meet *you*. You may feel as if you don't belong at your child's school or extracurricular events because such people have already been introduced to your child's "parents" and view you as an interloper.

Changing Your Child's Name

Following a divorce, a mother may begin using her maiden name or a new partner's last name as her child's last name. A father may do something similar, by referring to the child by a new nickname and/or only using *his* portion of a hyphenated last name.

Co-parents who try to induce loyalty conflicts in their children behave, in some ways, similarly to cult leaders (Baker 2007). They want their children to worship and follow them and only them. They want their children to show respect and allegiance to them and forgo all other important relationships. One of the first things that a cult leader typically does with a new member is assign that individual a new name. The reasons why cult leaders and some co-parents do this are the same: The act of naming a person is one of claiming ownership and authority, and it provides the person with a new identity. When a person enters a cult and has his name changed, he's being told, "You're no longer that other person with that other name who had those relationships and those beliefs and ties to the community. From this day forward, you're a new person with new beliefs and no ties to friends and family on the outside."

It's similar to telling the person that he's being reborn as a new person, with the cult leader as his parent. In a similar fashion, if your ex has begun to refer to your child by a new name, she's impressing upon him that he's no longer the same child who had certain beliefs and relationships. It's like wiping the slate clean, with your ex becoming the more important or perhaps only authority figure for your child.

If your child begins to refer to himself by this new name and claims that this is the way it has always been, you'll probably feel perturbed. You'll be placed in the position of having to either accept the new name—which carries with it your implicit approval of your ex's actions—or being in conflict with your child's stated desire to be called by that name, as well as your child's new version of his childhood, in which he has always been referred to by that name. If you refuse to accept the new name, it's likely that there'll be tension and acrimony between you and your child, who very well may feel hurt and misunderstood.

Rewriting History

Some co-parents try to make it seem as if before the divorce the other parent either wasn't very involved in their children's lives and upbringing or wasn't involved at all. Your ex may retell events from your child's early life in a way that casts you in a less loving or less active role than the one you actually played. Your child may come to believe that you rarely if ever fed him, changed his diaper, put him to bed, played with him, or had a hand in selecting schools, doctors, and so forth. Many of these early experiences are very important for children to know about. When children believe that they were well taken care of in their early life, they have a feeling of security about themselves and their relationships. And yet these memories are outside their actual ability to remember and know for themselves. They must depend on others to tell them who took care of them and how involved each parent was. If your ex repeatedly tells your child that you were disinterested and uninvolved during those early years, your child very well may believe it, and that belief might color his feelings toward you.

Your ex may go one step further and deliberately try to overwrite new experiences in order to reduce their impact and your role in your child's life. For example, if you buy your daughter a new dress, your ex might respond by buying one that your daughter likes even better so that she no longer has the memory of being excited about the dress *you* bought. Or if you take your child to see a movie or out to eat, your ex might take your child to the same movie or same restaurant in order to wipe away the memory your child has of being in that place with you. With memories of two similar events, the more recent or more impactful one may take precedence. In other words, if your child later thinks about that movie or that restaurant, she'll probably think back to the time that your ex took her, not the time that *you* did. The memory that's recalled more often is strengthened, while the other eventually fades.

Withholding Information

Erasing and replacing may also take the form of systematically excluding your name and contact information from your child's school enrollment forms, lists for team sports and other activities, medical records, and so forth. This means that if your child is injured or some other emergency arises during school or an extracurricular activity, you won't be notified. You won't be called when your child is hurt or in danger and needs you the most. You won't be invited to volunteer or attend social events related to the school, club, team, and so forth. You'll miss opportunities to forge connections with important people in your child's life and to show your child that you're a valued member of his community. Not being on distribution lists for important information may also cause you inconvenience. In one family of divorce, the father repeatedly removed the mother's name from school forms, denying her the opportunity to be notified of school closures (before such notifications became automated). More than once, this mother made the trek to her child's school during inclement weather unaware that school had been canceled. Yet another problem is that if your name and contact information aren't on class lists, team lists, and the like, then your child's teachers, coaches, and so on may perceive you to be an uninvolved parent and could possibly convey that impression to your child as well.

The more you miss out on, the more awkward it'll be for you to become involved in matters that concern your child. By the time you figure out when and where PTO meetings are held, for example, your ex may have already situated herself as the center of the social scene and made it difficult for you to feel that you have a right to be there.

If you're unaware of, and therefore miss, opportunities to attend events at your child's school and to watch your child's extracurricular activities, this could influence the way your child sees you and could confirm in the mind of your child the poisonous message that you don't care. Remember that children are egocentric and will assume that if one of their parents fails to show up at a game, an award ceremony, or a class play, it means that they, the children, are unloved. Missing these important events and moments in your child's life will deprive you of the opportunity to build shared memories. What your child will remember is that you weren't there. Any explanation for your absence that involves blaming your ex will likely fall on deaf ears.

It's sometimes difficult for others to understand and acknowledge what you and your child are going through. If you voice concern about your ex's "erasing and replacing" behaviors to a therapist, evaluator, or extended family member, this person may question your concern and wonder what your problem is with your ex trying to give your child experiences and material things that she desires. Divorce is commonplace, but alienation and loyalty conflicts are still often misunderstood. Others may not see how your ex is trying to reduce your significance in the eyes of your child. Your own friends and family may feel that what you see as your ex's attempts to steal your child are just part of the normal bickering of divorced parents. Mediators, therapists, evaluators, and judges may assume that you're engaging in similar behaviors to compete for your child's love or to try to get revenge. Unfortunately, in their denial and attempts to dismiss what they don't understand, they may inadvertently increase your frustration and feeling of isolation.

Is This Happening in Your Family?

Pay attention to how your ex refers to you when you're face-to-face, over the phone, and in writing. For example, when you call to speak to your child on the phone, does your ex tell your child, "Jane's on the phone?" Or when you arrive to pick your child up, does she say, "Let's go—James is waiting"? More subtly, does she fail to correct your child or discourage him when *he* refers to you by your first name?

Note that some young children go through a phase of using their parents' first names once they discover that their parents actually have names and aren't just "Mom" and "Dad." However, if your child refers to you by your first name but still calls your ex "Mom" or "Dad," and your ex doesn't seem to mind the double standard, you can be sure that your ex is using the strategy of referring to you by first name to induce a loyalty conflict.

A name change will become glaringly evident when your child refers to herself by a new name and insists that you do so as well. Again, a caveat is that some children go through a phase in which they experiment with different names. To rule out this possibility, look at whether your ex seems to have instigated the name change in order to exclude you from your child's life.

You'll know that your ex has installed a replacement when people in your child's community, like teachers or coaches, respond to your self-introduction as your child's parent with surprise, indicating that they thought they had already met the "real" parent. You might also detect this strategy if you hear or see your child referring to someone else as "Mom" or "Dad" in e-mails, on social media, in school reports, and so forth, or if he tells you outright that that's what he's doing. If you have questions about what is appropriate behavior for families with stepparents, you can refer to the book *Ex-Etiquette for Parents: Good Behavior After a Divorce or Separation* (Blackstone-Ford and Jupe 2004).

It also may come to your attention that virtually every time you take your child someplace fun or special or buy your child something, your ex is one step behind you, duplicating your actions. You may also hear your child talk about his childhood in a way that reflects a perception that you weren't present or involved.

Exercise 7.1: Is Your Ex Erasing and Replacing You?

Place a check mark in the corresponding column to indicate how frequently your ex exhibits the behaviors described since the divorce.

	Never That I'm Aware Of	**Sometimes**	**Often**
Referring to you by your first name			
Encouraging your child to refer to a significant other as "Mom" or "Dad"			
Referring to your child by a new name			
Not including your name on contact lists, school forms, and the like			
Retelling your child's history to minimize your role in it			

Common Responses That Do More Harm Than Good

If your ex is trying to erase and replace you, there are two major land mines for you to avoid:

- Responding with anger
- Assuming that your ex will include and involve you

The first mistake is for you to react with anger when you hear your child call you by your first name or refer to your ex's new partner as "Mom" or "Dad." Most children—whether or not they're experiencing a loyalty conflict involving their parents—are fascinated by their parents' anger and their own ability to push their parents' buttons. So, if you have a dramatic reaction when your child calls you by your first name or calls someone else "Mom" or "Dad," she'll probably do it again just to see your response.

The second mistake is for you to keep expecting your ex to include you in your child's academic and extracurricular life and reacting with surprise and hurt when that doesn't happen. Likewise, it would be a mistake for you to become angry at your ex when you discover that you have missed opportunities to be involved. Your child probably won't be receptive to finger-pointing and will assume that you—as the adult—are responsible for finding out what's going on at school, with the team, and so forth.

Suggested Responses

The first few times your child refers to you by your first name, although you may be surprised, try not to show any reaction. Play it cool and see whether the behavior stops by itself. If it doesn't, try making a polite request in which you explain how being referred to by first name makes you feel. For example: "Being your (mom/dad) is one of my favorite things, and I would really appreciate it if you went back to calling me ('Mom'/'Dad') instead of my first name.

Anybody can call me by my first name, but only you (and your siblings) can call me ('Mom'/'Dad'). Thanks so much." When you end with "Thanks so much," you show your child that you expect her cooperation. If your child goes back to using "Mom" or "Dad," show your appreciation and praise her for respecting your wishes. (See the seven elements of praise in chapter 4.) If your child continues to refer to you by your first name, politely remind her of your request. If the problem continues, try calmly *not* responding until she calls you "Mom" or "Dad," since ignoring undesirable behaviors can sometimes extinguish them; and if she complies with the request, respond quickly and positively. In other words, reward her with your attention when she does what you're asking of her.

I-Messages

When your child refers to you by first name and doesn't stop after a polite request, I-messages (introduced in chapter 4) may be appropriate. You might say: "When you call me by my first name, I feel disrespected. When speaking to me, please call me by the name you usually use." By using I-messages and polite requests, you focus on the impact of the unwanted behavior on your feelings. You're not telling your child that he's doing something wrong or bad, only that his behavior is making you feel uncomfortable. In this way, you model self-respect and help teach your child that feelings are never right or wrong—they just *are*. (See our discussion of emotion coaching in chapter 4.) In addition, you encourage your child to have empathy for you, which ultimately may make it more difficult for him to totally reject or discard you.

Exercise 7.2: Responding to Being Referred to By First Name

Using the following chart—complete copies of which can be found online at http://www.newharbinger.com/29583—or a similar format in a journal or notebook, keep track of how often your child refers to you by first name, your response, and what happened, in order to observe whether your response is working.

Date and Circumstances	**Your Response**	**Results**
Example: *We were in the store and Jake said, "Kevin, I don't like the shirt you picked out for me. Mom will buy my shirts."*	*I got my feelings hurt and felt pretty down the rest of the day. I couldn't shake the feeling that it was hopeless.*	*Jake seemed pretty smug at my gloomy mood, and I heard him talking to his mother, whispering about me. I think he called me a loser.*

Mutual Problem Solving

If your child reveals that your ex has been pressuring him to call you by your first name, to refer to his stepparent as "Mom" or "Dad," and so forth, you're in the fortunate position of being able to explore with your child ways to resist this kind of pressure.

First, be compassionate. Show your child that you understand his predicament—for example, "I imagine that it must be hard to have (Mom/Dad) ask you to do something like that." Ask your child what *he* thinks his choices are. Simply by asking the question, you plant the seed in his mind that he does in fact have choices and doesn't have to automatically do whatever your ex asks of him.

Your child might be able to think up choices and options himself, but if not, you can offer to brainstorm with him. One possibility might be for your child to write your ex a letter saying that he doesn't want to call you by your first name. Another approach might be for him to tell your ex, "I love you, but I also love (Mom/Dad) and I still want to call (him/her) (Mom/Dad)." A third option might be for him to relent and do what your ex is asking, even though it's hurtful to you. You can find more ideas for exploring options and discussing them with your child in *I Don't Want to Choose: How Middle School Kids Can Avoid Choosing One Parent over the Other* (Andre and Baker 2008). It's important for you to—as neutrally as possible—explore the advantages and disadvantages of these options with your child, and not appear to be rooting too hard for a particular one, even though in your heart you may very much want your child to choose that option.

If your child can come up with a solution on his own, it's more likely that he'll stick to it even if your ex tries to sway him. Moreover, your child will appreciate (on some level) that you respected his autonomy and allowed him the freedom to think things over for himself. Don't forget to show your appreciation for his efforts to resist pressure to choose between you and your ex. You might say: "I imagine that this may not be easy for you, and I really appreciate your willingness to explore some options that feel right for you. I'm impressed with your ability to come up with solutions and find one that works for you."

It may help your child understand your ex's actions if you put them in the context of how some parents behave during a difficult time such as after a divorce. For example: "Sometimes when moms and dads get divorced, they have a hard time sharing their children with the other parent. That doesn't make them a bad person. But they might do things to try to make their children think their other parent doesn't really love them or care about them. It can be tough for kids when that happens. Sometimes it's easier for kids to choose one parent over the other than to have to go back and forth and deal with that. I bet it's not always easy for you to go back and forth between two homes. Sometimes I or your (mom/dad) might ask you to do something that the other doesn't want you to do, and that can be confusing. But usually there's a way to work things out. If I ever do something that makes you feel as if you have to choose me over (Mommy/Daddy), please let me know. I really don't want to do anything that makes you feel that you have to pick me over (Mommy/Daddy). And, if (Mommy/Daddy) ever does something that makes you feel that you have to choose (him/her) over me, please remember that you really do not need to choose. You can love and be loved by both of your parents. If you ever feel otherwise, please remember to come and talk with me so that we can work together to find solutions that feel right for you. You're a smart and brave kid, and I know you can handle this." In this way, you're being compassionate with your child's struggle, and you're giving voice and words to what your child is probably going through, using emotion coaching techniques. You're also being encouraging, showing your belief in your child's ability to find solutions. You might add: "Please remember that you and I love each other and we need to be in each other's lives. What do you think are some ways you can remind yourself that you *do* love me, because it might be hard to remember sometimes?" It's good to ask this question, because the ideas that your child comes up with will be meaningful to him, and chances are good that he'll follow his own advice. It might also be helpful to have some ideas on hand in case your child needs prompting.

Tips: Helping Your Child Remember Your Love

Give your child a special piece of jewelry or some other token that reminds her of your love.

Place a loving card or note in your child's backpack.

Give your child a special picture of the two of you together for him to carry wherever he goes.

If your ex allows it, give your child two identical stuffed animals—one for each home—to remind your child of your love.

Come up with a special smile, wink, or hand signal (perhaps the American Sign Language sign for "I love you") by which you can show each other your love from a distance.

Put chocolate kisses in your child's backpack to symbolize your love for him.

Being Proactive and Involved

Responding to your ex's withholding of school, extracurricular, and medical information will require your vigilance. First and foremost, don't make any assumption that your ex will be providing you with information pertaining to your child. Go to the school yourself and make sure that your contact information is included on the forms. If it isn't, speak to the school administrators and have the forms changed to include your contact information. Bring a copy of your divorce decree or parenting plan in which you are designated as having some form of legal custody, if that's the case. If you don't have legal custody, check with an attorney about what rights you have to access school information. If you have some form of legal custody of your child, you're probably entitled by the Family Educational Rights and Privacy Act (FERPA) to be included on school forms and to have access to your child's school records. Without creating tension with school staff, let them know that you're an involved parent and you want what all legal custodians of children are entitled to by law.

Tips: Being Involved in Your Child's Education

Here are nine ways to be involved in your child's education (many from Epstein et al. 1997, noted with an asterisk) that don't require your ex's approval.

- Make sure that your contact information is correct in the school's database and that you know how to navigate the school's website (including the "parent portal").
- Be able to receive e-mail communications from your child's teachers, the school, and the district.*
- Meet your child's teachers, and attend parent-teacher conferences.
- Don't sit back and wait to hear from your ex or your child about what's going on at your child's school. Routinely find out for

yourself what's happening at the school. (And take this same approach with all aspects of your child's life).

- Show up for school events.
- Volunteer in the classroom, on field trips, and throughout the school.*
- Engage in home learning activities to support, consolidate, and enhance what your child is learning at school.*
- Volunteer on committees in the school and in the district.*
- Be an ambassador for the school in the community—speak well of the school, represent the school in community settings, and so on.*

When it comes to your ex rewriting history, if your child makes inaccurate statements that imply you were absent from her early life, gently correct the mistake. For example, "Actually I *was* there, and I recall…." If you can add a specific detail that will interest or amuse your child, all the better. If your child accuses you of showing a lack of care and attention toward her in her early life, the most meaningful response will involve compassion and active listening. Ask her what her thoughts and memories are and what it means for her to think that you weren't present or involved. For example: "So, you feel that I really wasn't around that much when you were a baby. How does that make you feel?" By giving her the opportunity to share her feelings, and by being compassionate toward her, you show her that you are—and thus probably always have been—an involved parent, whereas if you become angry, become defensive, or blame your ex, you demonstrate that your ex is probably right (in the mind of your child) in saying that you're unloving.

You can also mitigate your ex's rewriting of history by recalling and sharing, from time to time, warm memories of being with your child. Children are surprisingly able to absorb information that's presented as a story. For example:

- "I remember once when I was changing your diaper, the funniest thing happened..."
- "One night when you just would not fall asleep, I..."
- "You used to love your bath so much that I had to..."

You can also ask friends and family members who were present when your child was younger to recall for your child the bond between you and your child that your ex is trying to erase.

Exercise 7.3: Memories of Your Child

Use the following exercise to help you remember some important memories you have of your child so that you can share them with him or her when the time feels right. Record your answers in the following spaces, or in a journal or notebook. If you're co-parenting more than one child, you may want to complete this exercise separately for each child. You can download or print additional copies at http://www.newharbinger.com/29583.

Infant (birth to 1.5 years)

What was your child like during this time?

____

____

What specific memories of parenting do you have from this time?

____

____

Toddler (1.5 to 3 years)

What was your child like during this time?

____

____

What specific memories of parenting do you have from this time?

___

___

Preschooler/Kindergartner (3 to 6 years)

What was your child like during this time?

___

___

What specific memories of parenting do you have from this time?

___

___

Elementary Schooler (6 to 11 years)

What was your child like during this time?

___

___

What specific memories of parenting do you have from this time?

___

___

Middle Schooler (11 to 15 years)

What was your child like during this time?

___

___

What specific memories of parenting do you have from this time?

____

____

High Schooler (15 to 18 years)

What was your child like during this time?

____

____

What specific memories of parenting do you have from this time?

____

____

Fostering Critical-Thinking Skills

When dealing with your ex's efforts to minimize your role in your child's life, encourage your child to think for himself and to be aware of why he holds certain beliefs. For example, ask your child how he has come to believe that you weren't present or didn't participate in his childhood. (Be sure to ask these questions gently, or your child may feel attacked.) Most likely he'll respond, "(Mom/Dad) told me, and (she/he) never lies to me, so it must be true." Instead of calling your ex a liar, say something like the following, speaking in a calm and relaxed manner: "Sometimes people have different memories of the same event. (Mom/Dad) remembers it one way, and I remember it another. When two people have different memories, it doesn't have to mean that one person is lying. (Mom/Dad) wasn't always around, so (she/he) might have missed times when I was playing with you or taking care of you. For example, do you know that I used to pick you up from school every Tuesday when (she/he) worked late? Can you think of a time when you had a different memory than someone else and it turned out that your memory was mistaken or incorrect?" You might share a time when the same thing happened to you, in order to model the ability to reflect on your thinking and the ability to admit error.

Fostering Memories and Routines

Another strategy for responding to your ex's rewriting of history is to place photographs around the house that show you and your child together at various periods of her life. Refrain from pointing out, "See, we were close!" or "Your mother is telling lies. I *did* spend time with you." Instead, let the photos speak for themselves. If you put a photo of you and your child together on your refrigerator, your child will be reminded of that moment every time she gets something from the fridge, and she'll see for herself that you and she have a warmly shared history.

Yet another way to deal with having your past rewritten is to create and honor family traditions. If you and your child do certain things every year together—host a Valentine's Day party, watch the playoffs, volunteer at a charity on Christmas, see a movie on New Year's Day—it'll be harder for her to deny your involvement in her life because these times of year will serve as triggers of memories of your time together. You could aim to celebrate a tradition at least once a month in a way that you and your child look forward to and enjoy.

Exercise 7.4: Creating Family Traditions

Use the following table to help you come up with ideas for family traditions. Be sure to identify how your child can contribute in his own special way. For example, perhaps your child can decorate the Christmas cookies, set the table for the Thanksgiving feast, or create the invitations for the Chinese New Year's party.

Month	Your Family Tradition	Special Role Your Child Can Play
January		
February		
March		
April		
May		
June		
July		
August		
September		
October		
November		
December		

Another way to address your ex's rewriting history is to activate your child's sense memories. As in Marcel Proust's famous passage in *Remembrance of Things Past* about how the taste of a madeleine ("one of those squat, plump little cakes") unexpectedly evoked a time from his childhood (1981, 48–50), the senses—particularly the sense of smell—can activate deeply buried memories. If you used to take your child to a particular bakery and you recall having close and loving moments together there, bring her back to that bakery. Try not to make your intention in doing so obvious. For example, instead of saying "Do you smell this bakery? Doesn't that remind you of how many good times we used to have together here?"—which may seem manipulative—say: "I love coming to this bakery with you. We used to do this all the time when you were younger." This reflects love and appreciation, and celebrates the present as well as the past.

Gentle Corrections

When your ex makes comments that minimize your role in your child's life, you may feel such anger and frustration for the pain and suffering it causes to you and your child that you feel powerless to respond. In other words, the enormity of your ex's actions can be overwhelming. You also may believe that nothing you do or say can make a difference, since your ex seems so determined to steal your child from you. Despite these feelings, try to summon the strength and courage to show your child that it's possible to stand up to your ex in a dignified and rational way. Politely but firmly shake your head and say to your ex, "You know that's not true."

Tips: Respectfully Standing Up to Your Ex

Here are some more statements that can help you speak truth to power:

- "Just because you say something doesn't make it true."
- "I have my truth."
- "I was there, and I know how involved I was."
- "The kids know that I love them."
- "I wonder why you feel the need to say something that's not true and that could hurt the children."
- "If you're upset with me, please let me know that so we can talk about it away from the children."

Conclusion

Your ex may be trying to erase you from your child's heart and mind by demoting you from the role of parent, replacing you with someone else, changing your child's name, and withholding information from you. Your ex might also be minimizing your role in your child's development and trying to overwrite new memories that you make with your child. You can use I-messages to help your child develop compassion for you, and you can use polite requests to guide your child toward more respectful choices. You can gently and strategically set the record straight and encourage your child's use of critical-thinking skills, to help your child resist the pressure to reject you that she may be under from your ex.

8

When Your Ex Is Encouraging Your Child to Betray Your Trust

Betrayal of your trust refers to behaviors such as keeping secrets from you and spying on you. In this chapter, you'll learn how your ex might be encouraging this sort of behavior in your child, how that affects your child, and how to respond with mindful and positive parenting.

The Effects of Encouraging Your Child to Betray Your Trust

Your child wants her thoughts and her behaviors to be consistent. If she treats you badly, she'll want to believe that it's because you deserved it so that she doesn't have to feel guilty or confused about her behavior. In other words, your child will feel it necessary to focus on your negative qualities, in order to justify her actions. The unconscious thought process goes something like this: *It makes me feel uncomfortable to think that I, as a good person, did something to hurt (Mom/Dad), who's also a good person. I don't want to feel badly about myself. I'll change my belief that (Mom/Dad) is good. If I believe that (Mom/Dad) is actually bad, then (Mom/Dad) deserved the bad things I did. Therefore, I'm not a bad person for doing what I did.*

If your child can convince herself that you did something to deserve her betrayal, then she doesn't have to feel badly about herself or her behavior. In this way, your ex's enticing your child to betray you will set off a chain reaction in your child that increases the likelihood that she'll continue to reject and betray you in the future.

When you realize that your child has betrayed your trust, you'll probably feel hurt and angry, which will make it harder for you to make good parenting and disciplinary choices. Most likely you'll make choices that are counterproductive and could further entrench your child's alignment with your ex. When your relationship with your child becomes conflict ridden and emotionally compromised as a result, your ex reaps the benefits.

Your ex may set the stage for your child to betray your trust in one or more of the following ways.

Allowing Your Child to Choose Whether to Spend Time with You

Rather than respecting your parenting time per the court order, your ex may present spending time with you as an option, and not a very good one at that. For example, if your ex has to go away overnight during her parenting time, rather than informing your child that he'll be spending an extra night with you (assuming that right of first refusal—ROFR—is written into your agreement), she may ask him whether he would like to have a sleepover at his best friend's. (If you have right of first refusal, there should be no discussion of options; any time that your ex is unavailable is *your* parenting time.) Or your ex may entice your child to refuse scheduled time with you (as opposed to extra, vis-à-vis ROFR) by offering highly desirable alternatives—for example, "If you stay home this weekend, we can see a Broadway show and then go shopping!"

By creating situations in which your child is likely to select an alternative to spending time with you, your ex makes you seem expendable. The act of choosing creates a mind-set in which your child comes to see you as someone whom she doesn't care all that much about.

This kind of blatant pressure to choose works best with very young children, because they're generally more naïve and trusting. They typically have difficulty remembering their good feelings and loyalty toward the absent parent—in this case, you. Your child may be more easily swayed by the parent right in front of him (i.e., your ex) who's enticing him with "reasons" to forego visitation. Older children, however, are also susceptible to this kind of manipulation, because they typically have many material desires with which they can be distracted or bribed. Moreover, they can be seduced with non-material enticements, such as greater freedoms and privileges—being allowed to have boyfriends or girlfriends over to the house, a later curfew, less supervision and monitoring, and so on). If your ex presents herself as the parent who trusts your child to make his own scheduling decisions, your child will be flattered and will want to stay with her simply to have the experience of choice. Your ex may emphasize the unfairness of your child not having "a voice" in his schedule and cast herself as the parent who understands how mature your child is and how able he is to make choices for himself.

In extreme cases, a toxic co-parent may lure a child into requesting a change in custody. For example, "If you live with me, I'll have enough money to buy you a horse." Or "If you really loved me, you would stay with me instead of visiting your (father/mother)." Some co-parents believe that the court is unlikely to enforce parenting plans for children who are older or children who are particularly adamant about refusing visitation. It's true that family courts don't always punish co-parents for failing to follow court orders. In addition, some co-parents know that the other parent doesn't have the money or the wherewithal (enough energy and hope, access to good legal advice) to go back to court, so they feel emboldened to violate the order. As some co-parents with a toxic ex find out, once their child makes a "choice," the new schedule can become the de facto parenting plan.

Your ex may also allow your child to choose which parent to stand or sit near in situations in which both you and your ex are present, such as school or athletic events. When your ex refuses to stand or sit near you, he creates a situation in which your child has to slight one of you. Whichever parent your child approaches first has the advantage of appearing to have been chosen and preferred by the child. If your ex is able to induce your child to come to him first, your child might come to believe that your ex is the favored parent, in order to align his feelings with his behaviors. He might think, *If I always go to my father first, it must be because he's the better parent*, not realizing that he's actually been responding to subtle pressure and manipulation.

Forcing Your Child to Reject You

Some toxic co-parents will go one step further than allowing their children to choose not to spend time with the other parent. They'll have their children deliver the unwelcome news themselves. If your ex is forcing your child to reject you, your *child* will make the call to tell you not to pick him up next weekend because he doesn't like the way your home smells; *he'll* write the e-mail informing you that he's not comfortable with you attending his awards ceremony since you didn't pay for his uniform; and *he'll* be the one to text you to stop watching his baseball games because you are staring at him and everyone says it's creepy. Hearing such things from your child hurts even more than hearing them from your ex.

In one family of divorce, the father had the daughter write a note saying that she wouldn't be returning to the mother the following Monday as scheduled. He then drove the daughter to the mother's home and told her to slip the note under the door—even though the mother was home. As a final blow, the note was addressed to "Mrs…" instead of "Mom." The mother was naturally quite hurt, ashamed, saddened, and angered by all this. As for the daughter, she strove to justify her cold treatment of her mother by focusing on her mother's flaws, entrenching her disaffection for her. If the father had written and delivered the note, these actions wouldn't have had as much of an impact on the daughter.

Asking Your Child to Spy on You

If your ex is particularly interested in knowing whether you have a new significant other, how you spend your money, or certain information related to the divorce or custody, she may have your child try to obtain information about your affairs in a number of ways, including:

- Going through your mail in order to ascertain whether you have recently been given a bonus or a pay raise
- Looking through your call log and text messages on a regular basis in order to determine with whom you're communicating
- Going through your files (paper or electronic) in order to access documents related to your finances, the divorce, your social relationships, and so forth
- Gathering data on your recent purchases, including the make and model of electronics, cars, and other items

In order to justify asking your child to engage in a patently inappropriate act, your ex must first create the impression that she (your ex) rightly deserves this information and only needs to ask your child to obtain it because you're unjustly withholding it. In other words, your child needs to be made to believe that he's being recruited to right a wrong; were you not so difficult or deceptive, you would have given your ex the information already. Your ex will probably use flattery and appeal to your child's desire to be viewed as mature and trustworthy. Afterward, your child may feel especially close to your ex when he delivers the report, as the two of them conspire to keep the spying a secret. Your ex will probably heap praise on your child for being so brave and smart for accomplishing this important task. Thus the emotional rewards, positive reinforcement, and boost in self-esteem your child receives for engaging in this act of betrayal are substantial.

Asking Your Child to Keep Secrets from You

Secrets that your ex might ask your child to keep from you until it's too late for you to do anything about it include the following:

- A change in schedule or parenting plan that you might object to
- A trip out of town, state, or country that you might object to
- Health problems your child has had that your ex doesn't want you to be informed of because it might make him look bad (e.g., your child has suffered from depression, injuries, poor dental hygiene)
- A new relationship, or a development in a relationship (such as moving in together)
- Your child changing schools
- Your child starting therapy

Your ex may want to keep you in the dark about things like changing schools and starting therapy so that she can establish relationships with teachers, counselors, and others before you have a chance to, which enables her to present *her* version of your family situation to them in a way that puts you at a disadvantage.

Most toxic co-parents induce their children to keep secrets by convincing them that their self-interest is at stake. Your ex may advise your child not to tell you that she plans to give him something he wants (like take him to Disneyworld), because you would try to deprive him of it (say, keep him from going on the trip). After being primed to feel hurt and angry with you for wanting to deprive him of something he wants, your child would be ready to betray your trust and willingly keep the secret.

Is This Happening in Your Family?

If your ex is allowing your child to choose not to spend time with you, your child may come to believe that he has the right and power to exercise control over his parenting plan. He may claim to want "to have a voice," "to be heard," or "to have a say in my own life," all with a certain touch of arrogance and righteous indignation that indicates a "borrowed scenario" (see chapter 2). Generally, if your ex is trying to turn your child against you, she'll only afford your child a choice when it's almost certain to result in his spending less time with you. Most likely, she would suddenly become committed to following the plan should he ask to spend *more* time with you.

You'll know when your ex is allowing your child to choose if you keep careful track of implementation of your parenting plan. You can keep a diary of your parenting time to see where you stand. (See exercise 6.1, "Monthly Diary of Your Parenting Time.") It helps to know what you're actually entitled to, including right of first refusal, as regards parenting time. If you have right of first refusal and your child inadvertently reveals that your ex went away on her time by saying something like "When (Mommy/Daddy) went away last Tuesday, I stayed at Melissa's house," your ex may be allowing your child to choose. Remember, however, that children aren't always accurate reporters of their daily activities, so don't jump to conclusions; if you think that your ex may be making decisions that affect your parenting time without consulting with you, ask your ex about it directly.

Obviously, your child may reveal to you that he was given a choice to visit but declined because he had something better to do—for example, "(Dad/Mom) said I could decide whether to be picked up by you last night or stay home and have a family fun movie night with (him/her)." If you monitor your child's electronic communications, you might also see text messages or e-mails between your child and your ex in which your ex makes offers to your child to entice him away from you.

When you and your ex are in the same location at the same time, pay attention to where you physically stand in relation to each other and by whose choice. Try to keep a diary of these situations and see whether there's a pattern that would reveal that your ex is encouraging betrayal of your trust. Also, try an experiment in which, if your ex always chooses to stand far away from you, you purposefully stand near him (but only if you can do so in a friendly, cooperative, and kind spirit). See how that feels for you and whether it makes things easier for your child. If your ex manages to move away from you despite your having moved closer, then you'll have an even clearer sense that your ex wants to keep the distance, even—perhaps especially—if that means that it places your child in a difficult situation. Self-awareness will be an important asset here, because it's possible that *you* are doing something to cause your child to approach your ex first. In order to determine who's driving this behavior in your child, take a good look at yourself and your behavior during the times that you and your ex are at the same event. You might consider asking a trusted friend to observe the interaction and provide you with objective feedback. You could also discuss it casually with your child by gently asking him whether you do anything that makes him uncomfortable when the three of you are together. That doesn't mean that you're empowering your child to dictate your behaviors or actions, but getting your child's perspective might afford you some insight. Be sure not to denigrate your ex during these conversations.

You'll know if your child is being forced to reject you when your child is the one to notify you of your exclusion from important events in his life. He'll be the one to come to the door, call, or text you to inform you about "his" choice to exclude you.

It may be harder to ascertain whether your child is spying on you. Nevertheless, you might have a sense that your drawers or mail are being rifled through. You might see your child snapping cell-phone pictures of your purchases, your home, your pets, or your friends and sending them to your ex. You might overhear your child reporting on your behaviors, purchases, and so forth with a sense of urgency and secrecy. Keep in mind that some children are nosy for their own reasons. Spying only reflects a loyalty conflict if your ex is instigating (and gaining from) it.

Likewise, it may be difficult to know whether your child is keeping a secret from you. Eventually, you may become aware that your child knew something that she didn't reveal to you even though it would have been helpful and you had a right to know about it. Most likely your child will act as if she has done nothing wrong or find some way to blame *you*. She might say, "If you weren't such a meanie, I would have told you." Part of what complicates matters is that your child can and maybe even should have some secrets from you—children don't necessarily share every thought and feeling with their parents. Keeping secrets is indicative of a loyalty conflict only if your ex and your child purposefully keep information from you that you have a right to know, such as regarding your child's health and welfare or pertaining to your parenting time.

Exercise 8.1: Is Your Ex Encouraging Your Child to Betray Your Trust?

Place a check mark in the corresponding column to indicate how frequently your ex exhibits the behaviors described since the divorce.

	Never That I'm Aware Of	**Sometimes**	**Often**
Allowing your child to choose whether to spend time with you on your parenting time			
Forcing your child to reject you			
Asking your child to spy on you in order to obtain information			

Asking your child to keep secrets from you about things you have a right to know about			

Common Responses That Do More Harm Than Good

If your ex is encouraging your child to betray your trust, there are two major land mines for you to avoid:

- Taking your anger out on your child
- Focusing on the wrong thing

A primary mistake with respect to betrayal of your trust is to focus your anger on your child. This is an easy trap to fall into, because it's your *child* who's actively choosing your ex, rejecting you, spying on you, and keeping secrets from you. However, to take out your anger and frustration on your child—and to react to your child's outward behavior, rather than the way your child must be feeling—is to confirm in the mind of your child the poisonous message that you're unsafe, unloving, and unavailable. Co-parents who ground their child for a month for keeping a secret, call the police on their child for stealing their computer or breaking into their filing cabinet, or storm off in a huff when their child rebuffs them are falling into the trap that their ex has set for them. If you respond to your child with anger, you make it easier for him to justify what he did (*Mom's right—Dad really is a harsh and angry guy. He probably did keep those papers from Mom. I'm glad I could get them back for her.*) If you didn't have a toxic ex, there might not be any problem if you reacted in typical parent fashion and suspended certain privileges—say, grounded your child for a week—or confiscated a prized possession like an electronic game device or cell phone. However, even a routine punishment will only solidify your child's position against you.

Another reason to avoid a negative reaction is because you don't want to model for your child that it's acceptable to denigrate or devalue someone who has hurt her. If you come down hard on her for hurting you, you teach her to do the same toward you. Instead, show her through your example that it's possible to respond to people who hurt or disappoint her in a calm, rational, and loving manner; it's not necessary to devalue or discard people when there's conflict or disagreement. By treating her with respect despite her "bad" behavior, you model how you want her to treat you (and others).

Similarly, avoid becoming defeated and dejected by your child's obvious disrespect toward you and misguided loyalty toward your ex. You may feel like giving up, because while it's one thing to have your ex wage war against you perhaps by limiting your parenting time or cutting off your phone contact, it's another to have your child appear to be his willing and active ally. To see your child betray your trust and to justify amoral behavior can be quite disconcerting. You may wonder whether your child is already too far gone to feel your love and to know right from wrong anymore. It may feel as if you have already lost your child. Others in your situation have shared how disheartening it feels to see their child slip away, seeming to recognize no moral authority other than that of the other parent. But to give up or give in is to confirm in the mind of your child the poisonous message that you don't love him. If you want any hope of preserving a relationship with your child, you must summon your inner strength and respond to him with love, wisdom, and compassion.

Suggested Responses

You can use several of the positive and mindful parenting techniques presented in chapters 3 and 4 to help you respond calmly and lovingly to your child's betrayal of your trust.

I-Messages

Letting your child know how it makes you feel when he spies on you and keeps secrets from you can help you feel better and help your child behave better, so long as you do it with caution and restraint, keeping your child's age and developmental stage in mind, and with compassion in your heart. Speak calmly and respectfully. Be careful not to overwhelm your child with how much his behavior hurt, saddened, angered, or disappointed you; if you appear to be trying to crush his self-esteem, your child will most likely resent you for it. Likewise, if you share your feelings in a way that makes you seem excessively weak, dependent, or fragile, your child might be repulsed, be frightened, or perceive it as an attempt to manipulate him. Here are some examples of I-messages that might be helpful. Remember to follow an I-message with a polite and clear request about what you want to happen next time.

- "I feel confused as to why you went into my desk when I wasn't home. The next time that you want to see something of mine, please ask me."
- "When you kept your changing dance schools a secret from me, it hurt my feelings and inconvenienced me because I called the wrong place to get the schedule. If you know that I have the wrong information, it would help me if you could let me know. Thanks."

As in the first example, if your child is spying on you, invite your child to ask you directly for information. In this way, you remove the need for spying and show your child that you have nothing to hide. Point out, however, that some information may not be appropriate to share, and see whether your child can think of any reasons why. For example: "The next time you want to see something, just ask me. If I think it's appropriate for you to see it, then I'll be happy to show it to you. There may be some reason why I can't do that. Can you think of some information I would *not* be able to show you and why?" If you engage your child in identifying reasons, those reasons will make more sense to him than if you recite the reasons for him. However, here are some reasons that you may want to mention: the information pertains to someone else's privacy, or you have been ordered by the judge not to share the information.

Cultivating Compassion in Your Child

During discussions about betrayal of your trust, and over the course of your relationship with your child, try to elicit respect and compassion in your child by showing respect and compassion yourself. If you're harsh, sarcastic, or punitive, your child will only remember the negative quality of the interaction and not that you asked him not to go through your things or keep secrets from you. It might be helpful to follow an I-message with a positive statement that reinforces your child's moral and compassionate character, such as "One of the things that I love most about you is how you care about other people's feelings." Then insert a specific example from your child's life, such as "When you helped me fold the laundry when I was too tired to do it all myself, I was so proud of you. That's why I'm pointing out to you now how your (keeping a secret from me, spying on me) made me feel, because I know how much you value being a caring person."

Tips: Teaching Your Child Compassion

Here are some ways to help your child develop compassion for all living beings—not just you—so that she develops an identity as a compassionate person. The more compassionate she is and the more important it is for her to see herself as a compassionate person, the less likely she'll be to betray you in the future.

- Show compassion for her.
- Show compassion for other people you know.
- Get her involved in age-appropriate volunteer or charity work.

- Encourage her to donate her old clothes and toys to those less fortunate.
- Involve her in discussions of ethical dilemmas—what do you do if the cashier gives you back too much money, why tip a waitress, what should we do with clothes that we outgrow, why not to park in a handicapped parking spot, what to do with leftover food.
- Point out when people have been compassionate with her, and discuss how it made her feel.
- Praise and encourage her when she shows concern and compassion for others so that she incorporates concern and compassion into her core identity.
- Praise other people in front of her when they show compassion for others.

You can find additional ideas in *Calm and Compassionate Children: A Handbook* (Desmond 2007).

Mutual Problem Solving

Responding to your child's secret keeping can also include a discussion of different types of secrets. Explain to your child that you respect her as a separate person and, though of course you would be quite happy to hear her thoughts and feelings about any aspect of her life, you don't expect her to share everything with you. Ask her to think of some events or types of information that you would be okay with her choosing not to share with you, such as having a fight with a friend, reading a book that made her feel sad, or planning a surprise party for you. Ask her whether she knows why you wouldn't be hurt or angry if she chose not to tell you these things. Then ask her what kinds of things she should *not* keep a secret from you. Hopefully she'll list things like failing a test, having a stomachache, feeling really sad, taking something that didn't belong to her, and being bullied in school. Engage her in a discussion of why she shouldn't keep that kind of information a secret from you. In addition to mentioning how it would hurt your feelings or inconvenience you, focus on your role as her parent and the importance of having information about her well-being so that you can be the best possible parent to her. You might pose such questions as these:

- "Can you see how it would be hard for me to help you succeed in school if I don't know that math isn't going well for you?"
- "How can I protect you if I don't know that you're getting picked on?"
- "How can I make plans for us if I don't know when the schedule is being changed?"

In this way, you're showing her that keeping secrets makes it hard for you to help and protect *her*. As much as possible, try to keep the focus on *her* needs, not yours.

It's essential to *not* mention your ex or accuse her of manipulating your child and to speak to your child in a respectful tone that emphasizes mutual problem-solving. If you reprimand or lecture your child, she'll resent you for it and disregard your message. The objective is to have a respectful discussion about what is and what is not a safe secret. This could obviously prove helpful as your child matures, because other people may pressure her to engage in unsafe or secretive behavior.

Discussions with your child—about secrets, spying, and any other type of betrayal of your trust—will require a delicate attunement to your child. If your child agrees with you about any of the points you're making, he may feel as if he's betraying his other parent, the person who induced him to betray you in the first place. It's important that you do not in any way suggest that your ex is bad or wrong for having created this situation (not because this is necessarily the wrong message, but because it's not one that your child will be able to hear at this time). Throughout all of your discussions, try to convey that:

- Sometimes children whose parents are divorced feel that they have to choose one parent over the other, and this is normal. It doesn't mean that your child, you, or your ex is bad or evil.
- These situations can work themselves out, and the family will find a way to work together so that your child can love and be loved by both parents.

Even if you're certain that your ex is completely incapable of sharing your child, it won't be helpful to point this out—instead, show your child that you're willing and able to share him and that you hope that the same is true for your ex.

Cultivating Ethics

Another positive parenting approach to betrayal of your trust is to help your child develop an identity as an ethical person. If compassion creates an *emotional* motivation to refrain from betrayal, ethics provides the *intellectual* framework. Think of ethics as a moral code that you can teach your child over the course of her childhood. As with compassion, in your everyday interactions with your child, you can plant the seeds of ethical belief systems and work to create an environment and community that supports these belief systems.

The Josephson Institute's Six Pillars of Character

According to the Josephson Institute (2013), which promotes ethical decision making and ethical behavior, there are six pillars of character:

1. **Trustworthiness:** Don't cheat, lie, or steal. Be honest, reliable, and loyal.

2. **Respect:** Treat others with respect. Be tolerant of differences. Be polite and use good manners.
3. **Responsibility:** Do what you're supposed to do. Use self-control. Be self-disciplined and accountable for your choices.
4. **Fairness:** Play by the rules. Take turns and share.
5. **Caring:** Be kind and compassionate. Be grateful and forgiving. Help others in need; think about the needs and feelings of others.
6. **Citizenship:** Do your share. Be a good neighbor. Obey laws and rules. Respect authority.

Do your best to model these qualities yourself in your daily life, stimulate your child's desire to embody them, and praise and encourage her when she exhibits them.

Cultivating Compassion for Your Child

When dealing with any type of betrayal by your child, you may be tempted to view her as your abuser, someone who's acting badly toward you and bringing pain and suffering into your life. When you see yourself as a victim of your child's abusiveness, it's harder to use mindful and positive parenting. Therefore, you'll benefit from finding ways to work through your negative feelings in order to approach your child with compassion and a loving heart. Following are some suggestions.

First, remember the ways in which your ex manipulated *you* to go against your best interest so that you can empathize with your child, who's experiencing the same type of pressure. If you can understand what led you to fall in love with, start a family with, and remain with your ex for as long as you did, you can better understand what your child is going through.

Second, remember how important you are to your child, and allow yourself to feel sad for your child's loss of you, to whatever extent he's forgoing a relationship with you. Think about how sad it must be for your child to have to give up time with you and give up opportunities to be comforted, taught, and nurtured by you. Regardless of how blasé or cruel your child is being to you, what he really wants and needs is a relationship with you.

Third, to get a sense of the loss that your child is experiencing, remember how important your own parents were for you and the many ways in which they have been there for you throughout your life, to the extent that they have. Remember that all children want and need to be loved by their parents and that your child is being manipulated to cheat herself out of a loving relationship with you. Alternatively, think about the ways in which you wish your parents had been there for you, to remind yourself of how important parents are to their children.

Exercise 8.2: Ways Your Parents Supported/ Encouraged You

To help you remember the ways in which your own parents have supported you, think about each of the following categories. If you can, think back to the time when you were the age your child is now. In the following spaces or in a journal or notebook, write some of the most important examples from your childhood that pertain to each category.

Supported and encouraged academic success:

____

____

Supported and encouraged extracurricular activities:

____

____

Supported and encouraged social relationships and friendships:

____

____

Supported and encouraged relationships with extended family:

____

____

Provided necessary financial support and guidance:

____

____

Other:

____

____

Fourth, think about people inducted into a cult or a gang who relinquish friends, family, money, or a career in order to please the cult or gang leader. If adults can be enticed into going against their self-interest in order to please an authority figure who's merely a parent substitute, imagine how much harder it must be for your child to withstand the pressure being put upon her by an actual parent.

Fifth, if it pertains to you, think about how much difficulty you have had standing up to your own parents. Think about what you've been willing to give up—maybe the hobbies, friends, education, or career path you really wanted—in order to please your mother, your father, or both. Most people make some regrettable sacrifices to please their parents. Reminding yourself about that can help you empathize with your child.

Sixth, think about the ways in which you have been pressured, manipulated, or tricked by situations and people other than your parents and your ex. For example, did a friend once talk you into doing something you knew was wrong? Did you succumb to peer pressure at some point in your life and betray your ideals or moral values? Are you susceptible to advertising that convinces you that if you wear a certain brand of clothes or drink a certain flavor of soda you'll be surrounded by friends and feel happy and content? Have you mindlessly grabbed something off the shelf at the supermarket, without checking the nutrition label or price, simply because the packaging appealed to you? Have you bought something you didn't need, want, or use based on marketing or advertising, even if you couldn't afford it?

Reflecting on these points should help you stay mindfully attuned to the fact that your child is just a child—he doesn't have the cognitive maturity, the inner strength, or the specific skills (e.g., critical-thinking skills, assertiveness) to withstand pressure from your ex, even pressure to betray you and thereby betray himself.

Here are examples of thoughts that can help you remember that your child is a victim despite behaving like an abuser:

- *My daughter doesn't have the benefit of my helping her with math homework, which is something she probably needs. If she doesn't get the help she needs, her grades might suffer.*
- *My daughter hasn't been kissed goodnight by her mother (me) in three months. She must miss me so much.*
- *My son has been led to believe that his father (me) doesn't love him. That must really hurt him. What kind of father will* he *become?*
- *My darling daughter no longer trusts me, her father, to be safe with her in the car. That must be very confusing to her, because there's no basis in reality for this fear.*
- *My kids are being taught to be rude and careless. How will they be able to make and keep friends with that kind of attitude toward people?*
- *My daughter doesn't seem to care about anyone other than her mother. How will she separate from her to have a healthy life of her own?*

Exercise 8.3: Sacrifices Your Child Has Made for Your Ex

Try to think of the various sacrifices that your child has made in order to please and appease your ex. For example, has your child given up friends and hobbies, taken on unlikeable characteristics, or been untrue to himself in some important way? Write those sacrifices in the first column of the following chart. In the second column, write what you think the impact of that sacrifice on your child is. If you're co-parenting more than one child, you may want to complete this exercise separately for each child. You can download or print additional copies at http://www.newharbinger.com/29583.

What Your Child Has Sacrificed	The Effect on Your Child

It may help to refer to this chart when you're feeling most angry or annoyed with your child. With these thoughts in mind, you'll be able to respond to your child's betrayal with compassion and integrity.

If you punish your child for betraying your trust, only do so after a discussion of the problem and with a focus on the *behavior.* (Remember the four "Rs" of logical consequences: related, reasonable, revealed, and respectful—see chapter 4.) Avoid implying that your child is a bad person for having betrayed you. Perhaps you can share a time when you, unintentionally or because of prejudice or incorrect information, betrayed someone. Share how it made you feel, how you made it up to that person, and the moral lesson you learned from the experience. Remind yourself and your child that you love him, respect him, know that he's capable of doing better, and look forward to seeing an improvement in his behavior. Encourage him and bring out the best in him so that he'll still want to strive to please you and be his best self.

Conclusion

Your ex may create situations in which your child betrays your trust. Your child may spy on you, keep secrets from you, choose to not spend time with you, or reject you by excluding you from an important event in his life. Your child will be inclined to justify this behavior by blaming you for the betrayal. If your child can convince himself that you deserved this betrayal, then he doesn't have to feel badly about himself. Remember that your child is a victim, and try to cultivate compassion and an ethical awareness in your child so that he can withstand the pressure to betray you and so that you can respond to him with compassion when he does.

9

When Your Ex Is Undermining Your Authority and Fostering Dependency in Your Child

Your ex may be working to convince your child that she's the only parent whose opinion, approval, and authority matters by reinforcing the double message that your authority is invalid and that her approval is essential for your child's sense of self and well-being. In other words, your ex may behave both in ways that undermine your parental authority by encouraging your child to disregard or disrespect it, and in ways that foster dependency by inducing your child to rely on your ex as the sole parental authority. Your child may feel worried if she doesn't please and appease your ex—even when that entails behaving disrespectfully toward you or betraying her own best self. She may be willing to give up almost everything that matters to her in order to protect her relationship with your ex and to avoid what feels to her like the worst possible fate: your ex's disapproval and rejection of her.

In this chapter, you'll learn about specific behaviors that your ex might use to undermine your authority and encourage your child's dependency on him, how these things affect your relationship with your child, and what you can do about them. First we'll look at undermining your authority and then we'll look at fostering dependency in your child.

The Effects of Undermining Your Authority

Your ex may undermine your authority by creating rules of conduct for your child while she's with you. For example, you might offer your child certain foods, certain clothes, or the opportunity to participate in a certain game or activity, only to have your child decline because "(Mommy/Daddy) says I can't (eat/wear/do) that." Even if there's no apparent reason for such a rule—it's unrelated to health or safety and hasn't been deemed necessary by a relevant professional—your child may follow the rule regardless of the sacrifice, discomfort, or inconvenience involved and announce it to you without warning or consideration for your plans or desires. Following are two examples of co-parents imposing arbitrary rules of conduct.

- A father dictates how old his daughter needed to be before she could shave her legs.
- A mother restricts her son's diet even at his father's home, based on "food allergies" (even though no health care professional had determined he had any such allergies).

Another way of undermining your authority is disregarding rules that you have decided on together. For example, the two of you agreed not to show your son PG-13 movies until he's older but then your ex takes him to one, exclaiming that you're a "stick in the mud" for not wanting him to enjoy it. Your son now calls you a "stick in the mud" (a borrowed scenario) any time you try to enforce rules.

Yet another way to undermine your authority is to send your child to your home with food you don't want her to have, clothing you don't want her to wear, or something else that goes against your values. For example, in one family of divorce the father purchased a television set for the daughter to have at the mother's house—despite knowing that the mother didn't want her to have a TV in her bedroom. Your ex may leave brownies on your doorstep for your child when you're trying to limit sweets. Or your ex may send your child back to your house after a visit wearing what you consider to be inappropriate clothing.

It could also constitute undermining your authority if your ex commiserates with your child when your child calls to complain about a punishment or rule that you have imposed. If your ex responds as if you're being ridiculous or too harsh, your child will be encouraged to reject your discipline rather than learn from it. Your ex might blatantly encourage your child to disregard your restrictions and disciplinary measures and to view them as irrelevant and meaningless. Rather than learning the lessons you're trying to teach him, your child will learn that your authority is invalid.

If your child is older and is legally permitted to exercise her own parenting schedule, your ex may undermine your authority in another way: when you implement a punishment or try to make your child follow a responsibility like doing homework or chores, your ex "rescues" her by coming and picking her up, effectively ending your parenting time. If your child knows that you have no means of enforcing discipline because she doesn't have to stay with you, then you have lost the leverage that's sometimes necessary to hold your child accountable for her behavior.

In a related strategy, your ex may undercut your efforts to create a reward for a behavior that you're trying to foster in your child. For example, you inform your child that if she goes two weeks without a temper tantrum, you'll reward her with a new pair of shoes. Before your child has the opportunity to make an effort to control her temper, your ex goes out and buys her the shoes. In this way, your ex is telling your child that your system of rewards is meaningless and there's no point in striving to achieve the goals that you value for her. This is damaging to your parental authority.

It's also undermining if your ex enrolls your child in a new school, camp, therapy, or activity without discussing it with you or seeking your permission. Your child will receive the message that your input isn't relevant or desired and that you have nothing to contribute to his health, welfare, and well-being.

Yet another way to undermine your authority is to hijack your reasonably expected right to a special activity with your child. For example, most mothers assume that they'll be the one to purchase their daughter's first bra, while most fathers assume that they'll be the one to teach their son how to shave. Unless there's a good reason not to, your ex should respect your prerogative. In one family of divorce, the stepmother took the daughter to purchase her first bra when she was just five years old. Obviously, there was no need for this, and the act only functioned to demoralize the mother while demonstrating to the daughter which person would be playing the more central and gratifying role in her life.

Belittling and disregarding your values, norms, beliefs, and rules sends your child the message that you as a parent are irrelevant if not an annoyance to your child; the corollary is that your ex *is* a relevant authority—in fact, the only authority. It's not that your ex wants your child to disregard *all* authority; she just wants to invalidate *your* authority (and that of any other competitors for your child's affections and attention) so that your child will be more likely to respect her and not you. In addition to undermining your authority, your ex will do things that specifically elevate her authority, as described shortly.

The Effects of Fostering Dependency in Your Child

Your ex may emphasize his special knowledge of and insight into your child. He may make it seem as if he's the only one who truly loves and understands her. He may ask rhetorical questions like, "Where would you be without me?" Specific behaviors meant to reinforce him as your child's savior may include:

- Pointing out to her the times when he was right and she (and/or you) were wrong
- Recasting everyday events as situations in which he protected her or steered her in the right direction—for example,

convincing your child to not take part in a contest and then claiming to have prevented her from embarrassment or hurt

- Telling her that he knows which of her friends are "true" friends and encouraging her to cut off those he has decided have or will hurt her

Your child may be pressured to follow your ex's advice in every area of life and be rewarded for expressing gratitude for his supposed benevolence, keen insight, and ability to protect and guide her. The more often she expresses gratitude and acknowledges his unique and special role in her life, the more she'll actually feel it and come to rely on him. People generally come to believe that they mean what they are pressured to say, and children are no exception.

Your ex may try to insinuate himself into positions of authority in your child's community—for example, by coaching your child's sports team, volunteering in the classroom, or obtaining a high position in the parent-teacher organization. Needless to say, not every co-parent who volunteers or coaches is a toxic ex. However, a toxic ex is less likely to be satisfied with doing what he would consider to be thankless menial work. He'll want to shine and have authority over others in order to reinforce his importance to his child.

Your ex may belittle your child's coaches, tutors, teachers, and other authority figures he views as competitors for your child's affections and attention. He may come up with demeaning nicknames for them, mock them in front of your child, or explain to your child why they're foolish or misguided. He may encourage your child to see the worst in others and to feel entitled to look down on them as silly or cruel. Situations in which your child didn't get what she wanted (she wasn't cast as the lead in the play, for example, or didn't make captain of the team) may be portrayed as examples of other people's cruelty, as opposed to the result of logical or rational decisions. Your child may come to resent those who don't please her. She won't be inclined to want to please *them*, because she'll see them as capricious and ultimately unimportant to her long-term success. Should your child be given an honor or award, most likely your ex will take credit for it and expect your child to be grateful for his "essential" guidance and assistance.

Your ex may also act like a cult leader by using what's known as intermittent reinforcement to create anxiety in your child (Baker 2007). In this scenario, your ex normally showers your child with love and approval but periodically—and sometimes with no warning or apparent reason—behaves in a cold and aloof manner. When your ex withdraws his love, your child becomes preoccupied with winning his approval back at all costs. At these moments of vulnerability, your ex may extract promises from your child that further solidify his hold over her. He might require that she spend less time with you or forgo a hobby or activity in order to spend more time with him. Your child will experience such profound relief at being accepted back into your ex's good graces that she'll be even more enmeshed in and committed to that relationship. The experience of being temporarily cast out will have served to increase her sensitivity to your ex's moods and whims and heighten her fear of being in his disfavor in the future.

Your ex may presume to speak for your child and function as her agent and advocate. He may claim that your child isn't ready for overnight visits, isn't comfortable with you attending sporting events, doesn't feel safe with you driving her somewhere, or only wants to eat certain foods prepared in a certain way. In other words, your ex may act as if he knows and understands your child far better than you ever could, and as if your child doesn't feel safe or able to represent her own beliefs and desires to you. When your ex functions as a mediator between you and your child, he is preventing the two of you from having discussions and solving problems on your own.

Finally, your ex may try to convince your child that certain hobbies and friends are not good for him. By abusing her parental authority in this way, your ex may be able to override your child's own sense of what he enjoys and what he feels is right for him and reinforce the belief that without her, he would be subject to terrible harm and disappointment. Your child might say to himself that although he thought that a hobby was enjoyable or that a particular friend was a true friend, he was wrong and really can't trust his own perceptions. Your ex thereby undermines your child's critical-thinking skills and ability to know his own truth based on his own experiences and perceptions, with the result that your child grows increasingly dependent on your ex.

Is This Happening in Your Family?

You'll know when your authority is being undermined because you'll experience a loss of parental control and relevance. Your child will disregard your rules, appearing to care only about pleasing your ex and not about pleasing you or following your requests and household rules. You'll feel as if nothing you say matters and your child has decided that you have no means by which to enforce your parental authority.

In this situation, you should rule out developmental causes for your child's behaviors. Usually at least once during the teen years, a stormy child screams "You can't control me. You can't tell me what to do!" before slamming the front door as she races to a friend's house to complain about how horrible her parent is. What differentiates the normal Sturm und Drang of adolescence from the behavior of a child who's caught up in a loyalty conflict is that in the latter case, the disrespect and hostility are exhibited only toward one parent. Your child may still appear exquisitely conscientious about following your ex's rules, regulations, and even whims—politely if not obsequiously—never displaying to your ex the typical teenage drama of individuation and rebellion.

You'll know that your child is dependent on your ex when he appears willing to do, say, or try anything, follow any rules, and respect any regulations your ex wants him to. In everything he does, your child will appear to try first and foremost to please your ex.

Exercise 9.1: Is Your Ex Undermining Your Authority and Fostering Dependency in Your Child?

Place a check mark in the corresponding column to indicate how frequently your ex exhibits the behaviors described since the divorce.

	Never That I'm Aware Of	**Sometimes**	**Often**
Imposing rules for what your child can do and say even at *your* home			
Belittling your rules and regulations			
Commiserating with your child about your rules and regulations			
Making disparaging comments about other authority figures in your child's life			
Other:			

Common Responses That Do More Harm Than Good

If your ex is undermining your authority and fostering dependency in your child, there are two major land mines for you to avoid:

- Failing to love and accept your child for who she or he is right now
- Assuming that every decision your child makes is a reflection of your ex's manipulations

One of the worst mistakes you can make is to fail to accept and love your child for who she is. Your child may not be the person you thought she would be. Perhaps your ex has warped her opinions, attitudes, and maybe even physical appearance, or led her down a different path than she otherwise would have taken in her life. Perhaps your child was capable of excelling at hobbies that she gave up at your ex's urging. Perhaps she shows potential for academic excellence but struggles to pass her classes due to your ex's intrusions into her study habits and life choices. Perhaps your child could have been a compassionate person but instead has become strident and callous. Despite all the ways in which your child has been forced (and appeared willing) to alter her character and life course in order to please your ex, you'll benefit from being able to accept your child for who she is in the here and now. To hold on to the image of the child that you lost is to lose the person in front of you. Your child will sense your disappointment and will resent your shame about who she has become. She'll want to avoid spending time with you, because it makes her feel bad.

It's equally problematic to assume that every complaint your child has about a hobby, a friend, or you was planted by your ex rather than being an expression of your child's authentic thoughts and feelings. If you do this, you make yourself emotionally unavailable to your child, because you imply that she has nothing valid to say about her own experiences.

Suggested Responses

You can employ several positive and mindful parenting techniques in response to your ex's undermining your authority and encouraging your child's dependence on him.

Fostering Critical-Thinking Skills

If your child announces that he wants to quit a hobby, discontinue a friendship, or stop following an interest, and you feel fairly sure that he would be doing so to please your ex, explore that choice with him before it becomes a foregone conclusion. Skip the usual lecture in which you try to talk him out of it by pointing out how much pleasure he has gotten from that hobby, friendship, or interest; how committed he has been up until now; the advantages of sticking with it; and how little sense it makes to walk away at this point. Instead, in a very calm and neutral manner in which you don't appear to have a vested interest in the outcome, ask him to share his thoughts and feelings with you. Should he present a litany of "reasons" for his choice or complaints about the hobby, friendship, or interest, listen actively (see chapter 4) to try to understand his perspective. If what he says makes little or no sense to you, use a Socratic approach to try to spark his critical-thinking skills. Here are some examples:

- "What would your friend Sally say about the complaints you have about her? What do you think her side of the story is?"

- "So you want to give up the trombone after playing it for five years? What would you say to your friend if he told you he was giving up *his* favorite hobby?"
- "Would you like to make a list of the pluses and minuses of this choice, to make sure you're considering all the angles here?"
- "You're a smart kid, and I know you like to think things through. What are some of the things you have considered in coming to this decision?"
- "What would your music teacher say are the reasons *not* to stop playing?"
- "What would happen if you waited one month and then decided? Would you be willing to see how you feel then? Can you imagine that you might feel differently than you do now?"
- "What, if anything, would make the situation feel right for you? What would need to change for you to stick with your friend?"
- "Where do you want to be five years from now, and how—if at all—will giving up this hobby help you achieve your goals? I know that you have done some real thinking about this, and I'm interested to hear how you have worked this out in your mind."
- "What are some things you might want to consider before giving up a hobby?"
- "How do you know whether you're making the right choice and a good decision for you? What are some of the signs that a decision is a good one?"

This approach might result in a reversal of the decision, but if not, at least you will have demonstrated your commitment to your child's best thinking and to his welfare. Keep in mind that if during the discussion you come off as having a vested interest in the outcome, your child may feel as if you care more about some vision of him than about developing his autonomy—that you only love him when he does what you want. If you show real interest in his thinking and his experience, it's more likely that he'll feel validated and understood, and the door will remain open for future discussions about choices.

Accepting Your Child

If your child has already made decisions that you believe were based on manipulation and pressure by your ex, there's nothing you can do about that now. At this point, your task is to accept and love your child for who she is, even if she's a very different person than the one she might have been were it not for your ex's unhealthy and undue influence.

It may not be easy for you to accept your child this way. One way to work through your feelings of loss for the person your child might have become is to think about how you would feel if she was in a catastrophic car accident that forever altered who she was in some very significant ways. As painful as this exercise may be, it may help you find your way through the fog of unrealized expectations. Ask yourself whether you would still love and accept your child under those circumstances. Then ask yourself whether you would still be able to love and accept your child if she had been abducted or joined a cult for ten years and appeared to be irrevocably changed by the experience.

There are many reasons why our children don't turn out the way we hoped that they would. The malicious intrusion of a toxic ex is just one. Regardless of the past, unless you have a time machine, the only version of your child that you have the opportunity to have a relationship with is the one in front of you. We only walk down this path of life once, and in that sense we must play the hand we're dealt, no matter how frustrating and saddening that may be.

Tips: Practicing Acceptance of Your Child

Accepting your child just the way he is may be highly challenging. The following emotional exercises can help you stay in touch with the love that you have for your child no matter how different he is from your ideal.

- Develop a mantra to remind yourself of your love for your child. For example, "I love my child for who she is, just as she is."
- Read the chapter "Children" from *The Prophet* by Kahlil Gibran (1923), or listen to the song "On Children" by the singing group Sweet Honey in the Rock (both are easily found on the Internet). Consider in particular Gibran's line "Your children are not your children. They're the sons and daughters of life's longing for itself."
- Meditate and engage in other mindful activities to help you stay focused on the present as a way to keep regret and lost hope from overwhelming you.
- Reflect on an image of your child as a radiant and innocent baby who needs your love and acceptance.
- Focus on the positive aspects of your child's personality and strengths in order to truly appreciate them.

Exercise 9.2: Accepting and Appreciating Your Child

If you're co-parenting more than one child, you may want to complete this exercise separately for each child. You can download or print additional copies at http://www.newharbinger.com/29583.

In the spaces below or in a journal or notebook, list strengths and qualities your child has that you admire.

____

____

____

Now list some specific ways that you can show your appreciation of your child.

____

____

____

Forgiving Your Child

Co-parenting with a toxic ex means suffering many indignities and enduring many frustrating experiences; and because your child may at times appear to play an active role in your pain, you may need to forgive her for the ways in which she has and will hurt and frustrate you. You'll need to cultivate the art of forgiveness under such circumstances, because it may not come easily or naturally.

The purpose of forgiveness isn't to deny the pain that you have suffered, or to relieve the one who hurt you of responsibility, but to free yourself from the paralysis that comes from holding on to your anger and frustration.

Tips: Practicing Forgiveness of Your Child

Find a quote about forgiveness that speaks to your heart, such as "To forgive is the highest, most beautiful form of love. In return, you'll receive untold peace and happiness" (attributed to Robert Muller). Place it by your bedside so that you can see it every day.

Remind yourself that your child is a victim of parental alienation, which is a form of emotional abuse.

Write down all your angry, bitter thoughts about your child, and place them in a box to symbolize "putting them away."

Hold a forgiveness ceremony in which you symbolically discard your resentment and anger toward your child. This could be any act that symbolizes letting go of your anger. You might write your angry thoughts on a piece of paper and then either burn the paper or bury it and plant flowers on top of it. Or you might pretend your child is standing in front of you and say out loud that you forgive him.

From a spiritual perspective, you might want to forgive not only your child (who is, after all, a victim in this family tragedy) but also your ex—the one ultimately responsible for your pain and suffering—so that you can free yourself from the anger and bitterness that this person has brought into your life. Only you can know whether this is something worth exploring. If it is, you might want to consider the Buddhist prayer of loving-kindness. (There are many variations of this prayer, but all involve a wish for the other person to feel and know peace, to have an open heart, and to be safe.) You can also remind yourself of the course of events that led this person to feel so insecure, vulnerable, and/or angry that he feels the need to punish you and control your child.

Loving-Kindness

If you regularly practice forgiving your child in your heart, then you can more easily respond to him with loving-kindness when he behaves poorly. If your child yells at you, throws something at you, disrespects you, or disregards your feelings, try taking a mindful approach and asking your child what he's trying to tell you with his behavior. For example:

- "When you throw your toy at me, you're trying to tell me something about what you're feeling. Can you tell me with words, so that we can share this feeling together?"
- "When you don't follow rules that we have made together, I think you're telling me that the rules aren't important. I wonder what that feels like for you. What would it be like to have *no* rules? Should we explore that together?"

By not reacting to the *behavior* as the problem ("How dare you talk to me in that tone, young lady?"), you leave the door open for a deeper connection with your child. You're trying to speak to her with your heart in a way that invites her to feel your love and concern. You can always address her "bad" behavior with

I-messages—or consequences, if you feel that it's important to do so—at another time.

There'll also be times when you simply must say no to your child, yet you might hesitate to do so for fear of a defiant or disrespectful response or of widening the gulf of alienation that already exists. It might be helpful to find ways of saying no that are as compassionate as possible.

Tips: Alternatives to "No"

The following examples illustrate some alternatives to an absolute "No," which may sometimes feel harsh to your child.

- When your child asks to go to the movies: "I wish you could go to the movies now, but that isn't possible."
- When your child asks to go sledding: "Maybe we can go sledding another time, but right now it's time to…"
- When your child asks to be allowed to go play: "When you're done with your chores, then you can go play."
- When your child asks you to leave the light on at bedtime: "Going to bed with your light on might keep you up. Can you tell me about why you're asking for that?"
- When your child asks whether she can do a different chore than washing dishes this week: "We have already decided that the dishes are your chore for the week, but perhaps you want to want to put a discussion of changing chores on the agenda for the next family meeting."
- When your child requests noodles for lunch and you don't have any: "There are no more noodles in the house right now. Your choices for lunch are…"

Explore your own reasons for saying no. Sometimes as parents we assume that the response to certain unusual requests, such as to be allowed to eat noodles for breakfast, wear pajamas all day, or read in bed with a flashlight, must be no. However, it helps avoid unnecessary conflict and bad feelings if you're willing to examine some of your assumptions before automatically saying no. If you can't think of a good reason, for the sake of your child's learning and growth, perhaps it's worth a try. You can always add a qualifier, such as "Let's see how it works and then discuss it again in a week," to give yourself the opportunity to revisit the decision should it turn out that there *was* a good reason to say no after all.

Mutual Problem Solving

Sometimes children resist rules because they don't understand them. If your child doesn't understand the reasoning behind some of your rules, your ex may be able to easily convince him to disregard or rebel against them. In order to avoid this problem, try not imposing a rule on your child before engaging him in a conversation in which you ask him *why* he thinks you're concerned about whatever it is that you want to create a rule about—say video games, bedtime, or baths. You could even try to make it fun by challenging him to come up with as many reasons as possible or paying him a quarter for every reason he can offer. Once he has identified some reasons, ask him what he thinks would be a fair way to resolve the issue. He might come up with a creative solution that you hadn't considered, or at least one that's consistent with your values. If the solution you decide on together is one that he came up with himself, he's much more likely to respect it and will be less inclined to let your ex undermine it.

If your child misbehaves and you must impose a consequence, we advise that first you do some mutual problem solving. If you give your child an opportunity to explain his thoughts and feelings and engage him in a reasoned and respectful discussion of possible solutions, the problem can be resolved in a way that works for everyone. Because the decision will be a shared one, your child will be less likely to complain about it to your ex or rebel against it. For example, if your child broke a window in the house, rather than immediately responding with a consequence, explore with your child how it happened. Perhaps you'll learn that your child was upset about something at school, or perhaps he needs more opportunities to exercise and release pent-up energy. Once you have an understanding of the underlying causes (and hopefully some ideas about how to address them), invite your child to help you brainstorm possible solutions. Anything that your child comes up with that's acceptable to you is great. If he doesn't have any ideas, you can offer a few, such as having a bake sale to raise money to cover the cost of a replacement window. The key is to be flexible, open-minded, and appreciative of your child's involvement in the discussion. In this way, you reward him for pro-social behavior, and you reinforce your respect for him and the importance of the process. It's not so much *what* decision is made but *how* it's made. Once you have arrived at a decision together, praise your child (remember the seven elements of praise in chapter 4) for his cooperation and ability to work through problems. This reinforces his identity as a problem solver.

Identifying Goals and Aspirations

While your child may appear to live in service of pleasing your ex, there still may be a way to keep him from turning his back on talents, hobbies, friends, and dreams that don't conform to your ex's plans for him. One way to do that is to engage your child in discussions about his long-term goals. If he can develop his own goals, he may be less likely to disown them when your ex pressures him to do so. From time to time, talk with your child about where he sees himself next year, in five years, and in ten years. Discuss what he needs to do to reach his goals, emphasizing that his goals are his own. Make a list of his goals, plans, and dreams, post it on the fridge or in his room, and encourage him to achieve them. Show him that you believe in him and know that he's smart and hardworking and will be able to achieve his aspirations.

Conclusion

If your ex is trying to turn your child against you, she may undermine your authority and act as though *she's* the primary, if not exclusive, authority over your child. Rather than encouraging your child to think for himself and know his own truth, your ex may tout herself as the person on whom your child should rely at all times. Your task remains to help your child know himself, be true to himself, and strive to achieve his goals. You'll need to bring your best parenting to the fore to create a strong foundation that supports your child's identity as a separate person who can love and be loved by both parents. Mutual problem solving is a vital parenting strategy in this situation. When your child participates in discussions of rules and helps identify solutions to problems, he'll be less susceptible to your ex's interference and intrusion.

Final Words

We encourage you to ponder these questions to find your own truth:

- How can I remember that my child is a victim when she's treating me so badly and causing me so much pain and suffering?
- How can I better practice mindfulness so that I can cherish the time that I have with my child?
- How can I avoid the traps of anger and defeat?
- How can I help my friends and family understand my situation better?
- What other support do I need during this time?
- How can I stay true to my values while being undermined and denigrated?
- What messages is my child receiving about me, and how can I "be" the message that I want my child to receive?
- How can I cultivate compassion in both myself and my child?
- How can I instill ethical ideals in my family?

- What images do I hold in my mind and heart that interfere with my ability to be present for my child?
- How can I best speak truth to power so that I don't feel powerless and invisible to my child?
- How can I be mindful and awake to the precious gift of my child?

We encourage you to refer back to this book often on your journey through life as a co-parent with a toxic ex. We hope that each time you revisit a chapter or a section of the book, you find or are reminded of something that helps you stay strong, be true to yourself, and be the best possible parent to your child. Be sure to keep in mind that your child needs and loves you more than he can let you know.

References

Adler, A. 1927. *The Practice and Theory of Individual Psychology.* Eastwood, CT: Martino Fine Books.

Andre, K., and A. J. L. Baker. 2008. *I Don't Want to Choose: How Middle School Kids Can Avoid Choosing One Parent over the Other.* New York: Kindred Spirits.

Baker, A. J. L. 2007. *Adult Children of Parental Alienation Syndrome: Breaking the Ties That Bind.* New York: W. W. Norton.

———. 2010. "Even When You Win You Lose: Targeted Parents' Perceptions of Their Attorneys." *American Journal of Family Therapy* 38 (4): 292–309.

Baker, A. J. L., and N. Ben-Ami. 2011. "To Turn a Child Against a Parent Is to Turn a Child Against Himself." *Journal of Divorce and Remarriage* 52 (7): 472–89.

Baker, A. J. L., B. Burkhard, and J. Kelly. 2012. "Differentiating Alienated from Not Alienated Children: A Pilot Study." *Journal of Divorce and Remarriage* 53 (3): 178–93.

Baker, A. J. L., and J. Chambers. 2011. "Adult Recall of Childhood Exposure to Parental Conflict: Unpacking the Black Box of Parental Alienation." *Journal of Divorce and Remarriage* 52 (1): 55–76.

Baker, A. J. L., and D. Darnall. 2006. "Behaviors and Strategies Employed in Parental Alienation: A Survey of Parental

Experiences." *Journal of Divorce and Remarriage* 45 (1–2): 97–124.

———. 2007. "A Construct Study of the Eight Symptoms of Severe Parental Alienation Syndrome: A Survey of Parental Experiences." *Journal of Divorce and Remarriage* 47 (1–2): 55–75.

Baumrind, D. 1966. "Effects of Authoritative Parental Control on Child Behavior." *Child Development* 37 (4): 887–907.

Bernet, W., W. V. Boch-Galhau, A. J. L. Baker, and S. Morrison. 2010. "Parental Alienation, DSM-V, and ICD-11." *American Journal of Family Therapy* 38 (2): 76–187.

Blackstone-Ford, J., and S. Jupe. 2004. *Ex-etiquette for Parents: Good Behavior After a Divorce or Separation*. Chicago: Chicago Review Press.

Blau, M. 1993. *Families Apart: Ten Keys to Successful Co-parenting.* New York: G. P. Putnam's Sons.

Briere, J. 1992. *Child Abuse Trauma: Theory and Treatment of the Lasting Effects*. Newbury Park, CA: Sage Publications.

Ceci, S. J., and M. Bruck. 1993. "Suggestibility of the Child Witness: An Historical Review and Synthesis." *Psychological Bulletin* 113 (3): 403–39.

Center for the Improvement of Child Caring. 2001. *Confident Parenting: Contemporary Skills and Techniques for Achieving Harmony in the Home*. Studio City, CA: Author.

Dermond, S. U. 2007. *Calm and Compassionate Children: A Handbook*. Berkeley, CA: Celestial Arts.

Dreikurs, R. 1991. *Children: The Challenge*. New York: Plume.

Duncan, L. G., J. D. Coatsworth, and M. T. Greenberg. 2009. "A Model of Mindful Parenting: Implications for Parent-Child Relationships and Prevention Research." *Clinical Child and Family Psychology Review* 12 (3): 255–70.

Dutton, D. G., and S. L. Painter. 1981. "Traumatic Bonding: The Development of Emotional Attachments in Battered Women and Other Relationships of Intermittent Abuse." *Victimology: An International Journal* 6 (1–4): 139–55.

Epstein, J. L., M. G. Saunders, S. B. Sheldon, B. S. Simon, K. C. Salinas, et al. 1997. *School, Family, and Community Partnerships: Your Handbook for Action*. Thousand Oaks, CA: Corwin Press.

Gardner, R. A. 1998. *The Parental Alienation Syndrome: A Guide for Mental Health and Legal Professionals*. Cresskill, NJ: Creative Therapeutics.

Gibran, K. 1923. *The Prophet*. New York: Alfred A. Knopf.

Gordon, T. 1970. *Parent Effectiveness Training*. New York: Three Rivers Press.

Gottman, J. 1998. *Raising an Emotionally Intelligent Child*. New York: Simon and Schuster.

Kabat-Zinn, J. 2003. "Mindfulness-Based Interventions in Context: Past, Present, and Future." *Clinical Psychology: Science and Practice* 10 (2): 144–56.

Kabat-Zinn, M., and J. Kabat-Zinn. 1997. *Everyday Blessings: The Inner Work of Mindful Parenting*. New York: Hyperion.

Kempe, R. S., and C. H. Kempe. 1978. *Child Abuse*. Cambridge, MA: Harvard University Press.

Josephson Institute. 2013. "The Six Pillars of Character." http://josephsoninstitute.org/sixpillars.html.

Loftus, E. 1997. "Creating False Memories." *Scientific American* 277 (3): 70–75.

Nelson, J. 2006. *Positive Discipline*. New York: Ballantine Books.

Popkin, M. 2002. *Active Parenting Now*. Marietta, GA: Active Parenting Publishers.

Proust, M. 1981. *Remembrance of Things Past, Vol. 1*. Translated by C. K. Scott Moncrieff and Terence Kilmartin. New York: Vintage Books.

Amy J. L. Baker, PhD, is a national expert on children caught in loyalty conflicts and has written a seminal book on the topic, *Adult Children of Parental Alienation Syndrome*, published by W.W. Norton and Company. In addition to conducting trainings around the country for parents as well as legal and mental health professionals, Baker has written dozens of scholarly articles on topics related to parent-child relationships and has appeared on national TV, including *Good Morning America*, CNN, and the *Joy Behar Show*. She has been quoted in the *New York Times* and *US News and World Report*, among other print media outlets. Baker graduated from Barnard College, summa cum laude and Phi Beta Kappa. She has a PhD in human development from Teachers College, Columbia University. More information is available on her website at www.amyjlbaker.com.

Paul R. Fine, LCSW, is a licensed clinical social worker and psychotherapist in practice at a community mental health center in northern New Jersey. He has over 25 years' experience working with diverse populations. His practice includes an eclectic and humanistic approach to problems faced by individuals and families.